IF YOU WANT TO
──── LIVE ────
MOVE!

Putting the Boom Back into Boomers

ELAINE LALANNE | JAIME BRENKUS

The information in this book reflects the author's experiences and opinions and is not intended to replace medical advice. Before beginning this or any nutritional or exercise regimen, consult your physician to be sure it is appropriate for you.

Elaine's Cover Photo by Steve Haining

Book design by Kelley Creative.
www.kelleycreative.design

ISBNs 978-0-578-43543-5, 978-1-688-79956-1

Table of Contents

FOREWORD

All my life I've looked for a role model… a woman I could emulate, hold to a high standard, who I could look up and know which way to go when the winds of life blew me off course. My mom, God rest her soul, was an amazing woman with a giving heart and a great laugh, but she outwardly fought her weight demons, had limiting beliefs about being an only child, and thought playing small was playing safe. I always found that frustrating. My grandmothers both passed shortly after I was born, and I'm the oldest girl of two in my family. My father was innovative, an inventor and magician. I learned a lot and dreamed a lot thanks to his coaching… but there was always an emptiness. A longing to find a female mentor who held a torch. Perhaps, I'm being a touch dramatic, but by my wanting it so much… she actually appeared!

In 2002, when I had just turned 42, after having lost both my parents at 70 to cancer and diabetes, I delivered my 7-pound boy/girl twins; healthy, vibrant miracles but they left me extremely overweight, saggy, feeling tired, and thinking in despair, that perhaps my tv hosting and fitness career was at an end.

Well, if you listen closely, they say, "When God closes a window, he opens a door."

And just like that, while nursing my twins and having been out of the work circuit for about 5 months (I had a 65-inch waistline and ballooned from 130lbs up to a 208), I got a call from my agent. He asked if I would head to Toronto, Canada to co-host a new Power Juicer infomercial with Elaine and Jack LaLanne.

My first instinct was to jump at the opportunity, then I realized not only couldn't I physically jump, I had trouble just getting out of bed. The offer to work with the mega fitness couple was scheduled for 9 weeks from then. I had a choice and chance to regain, or to lose everything. I Googled Jack LaLanne and my life was never the same. I thought I had an idea of who he was, I recognized the blue jumpsuit, had seen his name on health clubs growing up, and I remembered his white dogs that my mother loved when she would work out with him in the mornings.

And just 9 weeks later after an intense detox and fitness regime, I lost enough baby weight to brave a trip to Toronto that would truly be the greatest turning point in my infomercial hosting career.

When I first met Elaine and Jack in the Canadian dressing room, what stood out was their Jack and Jill relationship— how they finished each other's sentences, had an effervescent joy about them, and it truly seemed like they had been friends for years. The first Juicer Infomercial we shot that day was basically a conversation about food, nutrition, and life. Mostly unscripted—it went on to run for 8 years in 80 countries and grossed almost a billion dollars in sales. There was an honesty and curiosity and while Jack had a massive mission to pitch, Elaine and I had the time of our lives juicing, laughing and enrolling the world into the vision of health and fitness naturally.

I had the most magical time. Jack and Elaine got to meet my baby twins, and to this day, our photo is one of my all-time favorites.

I would raise my children with 3 of the principles I learned from the LaLanne's that truly shaped our lives from then on...

1. If man-made, don't eat it.

2. Exercise is King, nutrition is Queen, put them together and you've got a kingdom.

3. Ten seconds on the lips and a lifetime on the hips.

My family had the honor of waking up at Elaine and Jack's house on his 96th birthday. In fact, we celebrated eight of his birthdays with him and Elaine. I loved the way they looked at each other, held hands, and sang to one another. Imagine spending five decades growing, learning, and loving.

But what did Elaine do when Jack left? I'll tell you. She took all the spirit and love she has and began to truly give it back out to the world. I know she missed him, we all do—but she knows she has a mission left to do—and that is to continue to inspire us all. She walks the walk, and practices what she preaches. Elaine is a beacon of sunshine, energy, and optimism. I am beyond grateful to not only have worked with her, but to get close enough to be invited into her home, her family, and her heart.

I had an especially touching moment recently in her home with my 15-year-old daughter Makenna. It was magical to watch these two, who have almost an 80-year difference in ages, sit together and tell stories, laugh, and Elaine was even brave enough to let my daughter drive her car! We ate healthy food, talked about the power of juicing, and then Elaine hit the gym in her home and Makenna's jaw just dropped. A woman of 92 was doing pushups, leg lifts and hanging from a crossbar and doing stomach crunches! We are so blessed that she has once again agreed to put her secrets, tips and insights into a book. They say that "Youth is wasted on the young"—not in this case. Elaine is the embodiment of youth and vitality and thankfully she shares about how we too can attain and maintain that same energy.

Elaine LaLanne is truly "The First Lady of Fitness," and my role model as a mother, wife, spokesperson, and human being. I'm a much better person from nutrition to attitude because she is in my life and YOU will be a much better person when you read her book and follow her lifelong principles. But this book is not just hers, she has teamed up with fitness and nutritional expert, Jaime Brenkus, in their new book, "If You Want to Live, Move!". It's exciting because it focuses on how quick and easy it is, for anyone, at any age to get started—feeling and looking better. Age should never be a reason to not get started. Like Jack always said, "Life is great when you're in shape!".

LaLa, I love you!

Forbes Riley

Author, lifestyle expert and award winning TV host (over 15 years as host of the Jack LaLanne Juicer infomercials)

Jaime's Programs work...

As a sports medicine physician, one of the most difficult problems that I've had to deal with is weight loss. Obesity is truly an epidemic in this country leading to many other health problems, including hypertension, diabetes and low back pain. Unfortunately, there is no easy way to recommend weight loss to patients. Jaime's program is truly the finest weight management program that I have ever recommended.

It is precise, accurate and extremely effective. The program uses sound scientific principles to help people lose weight. I can recommend this program to any patient without reservation and know that they will be treated with kindness, respect and confidentiality. The results will speak for themselves.

Dr. Michael Kellis

Sports Medicine Director Geauga Regional Hospital, University Hospitals of Cleveland

It is never too late in life to make responsible lifestyle choices. In fact it is one of the most important steps you can take for healthy aging. As we age, proper nutrition becomes even more essential to good health, how we feel and can inspire a sense of well-being. Not only what you eat but how much you eat can be a powerful tool in controlling weight and more importantly health no matter what your age. You must be mindful of what you put on your plate and how you move your body. Good nutrition and physical activity go hand-in-hand in helping us to feel younger and healthier and to lower our risk for age-related health issues.

Reliable resources, such as "If You Want to Live... Move" are the perfect way to get all of the information you need at this stage of life. Don't let anyone but YOU control what your future brings!

Kimberly Tessmer, RDN, LD

Registered Dietitian, Health Coach and Published Author
www.Nutrifocus.net

ACKNOWLEDGEMENTS

Without Jaime Brenkus, and Charles Calise and Evergreen Wellness, I wouldn't be writing my acknowledgements, for they were instrumental in getting me on board for this book.

I would be remiss if I didn't mention my husband, Jack LaLanne, who was my mentor, my inspiration and my teacher and gave me the incentive to change my life at the age of 27 so I could live a prolonged healthy, life.

To Sandy Vettel, our editor, who kept us on the straight and narrow.

Gale Rudolph: To my friend, nutrition and food scientist, Dr. Gale Rudolph PH.D, CNS,FNS, who keeps me updated. She has worked with Jack and me for over 30 years since graduating from UCLA, in Los Angeles, and is always there for me when I have questions on nutrition.

To Forbes Riley, internationally known spokesperson, keynote speaker, author, lifestyle expert and award winning TV host (over 15 years as host of the Jack LaLanne Juicer info-mercials) for writing such a glowing forward for this book.

To Maria Shriver, who prompted me to write for her Sunday Online Paper three things that were instrumental in living a long productive life. I came up with "My ARC"; Attitude, Resistance, and Consistency.

To Rick Hersh, my agent who urged me to do this book.

To my supporters and those of you who have given me input and cheered me on.

My sons, Danny, Jon Allen and his wife Lora LaLanne, daughter Dr. Yvonne LaLanne and her husband Dr. Mark Rubenstein.

Denise Austin, Dan Isaacson, Kyltie and Brette Diggins, Sara Loven, Jeanine Victor, Claire Townsley, Cara Jacobsen, Maia Sotelo, Bruce Gaims, and for you the public who I have been in touch with through my career. A special thanks to Joon Oh, Brooks Wachtel, and John Cates.

I deeply thank all of you from the bottom of my 90-plus, "athletic" heart!

Elaine LaLanne

I want to thank my two favorite ladies, my loving wife, Teri, and my beautiful daughter, Lauren. You both are my daily driving force. Thanks Mom and Dad who continue to be an inspiration to me and are my biggest fans.

Thanks to Charles Calise and Courtney Peffley, and the entire Evergreen Wellness team for their shared vision to assist Baby Boomers in their most valued possession, their health. Thank you to our editor, Sandy Vettel, for your keen eye in making me cut, when I wanted to keep.

Special thanks to our favorite nutritionist and Chef extraordinaire, Dani Spies. We're privileged to have her scrumptious, clean and delicious recipes in our mix.

And a special thank you to the LaLanne family. Without Jack and Elaine's devoted dedication to the spirit of wellness and fitness, our industry would have never been as prominent in people's lives. They paved the way for me and every health and fitness professional to live their dream. With this book, I'm honored to be a part of that legacy. Working with Elaine this past year exemplifies what true passion and lifelong faithfulness to your lifestyle really means. Her energy is infectious. I couldn't keep up with all her ideas and creativity. It was truly an experience I'll never forget. I'm forever grateful!

Jaime Brenkus

INTRODUCTION

Hello, Boomers!!!

We're dedicating this book to you so you can get that old "boom" back. With over 100 years of fitness and nutrition experience combined, we knew as we rounded the corner to another year and another phase of our lives, we needed to write this book, *If You Want to Live, Move!* and share our best secrets and tips with our fellow boomers (and seniors!). We're keyed-up to show how you, too, can enjoy abundant strength, energy, flexibility and endurance to live a long, productive life which you richly deserve. We feel you are holding in your hands a prescription for ageless energy and timeless health.

We are fitness and nutrition professionals. As good fortune would have it, we stumbled upon the secret many, many years ago (it's not really a secret, as you will learn) of living a life of vitality, optimism and prime physical health.

One of us was born in 1926, and the other was born in 1961.

One of us lives on the west coast and one in the Midwest. One of us is a woman, one of us, a man.

One, a senior (from the greatest generation that ever lived), one a boomer.

On the surface, it appears we don't have much in common.

In fact, we have a lot in common; the most important is this:

We both have a passion for teaching others the right way to live fuller, richer lives!

You could say we both 'talk the talk' and 'walk the walk'. So, let us talk to you about a new beginning and walk you through it!

This book is about how to dig deep to create more energy, immense joy and better health.

It explores the intersection of fitness and aging, and ultimately answers these two questions:

- Is there a secret magic potion for living longer? (yes and no)

- Which is most important, diet or exercise, for feeling younger and being healthier? (both)

We put our brains together to come up with a plan for changing your life for the better.

In this book, you'll learn easy, effective ways to deal with difficult challenges we all face as we climb over the next hill, including low energy, increasing weight and sagging skin, achy bones and joints, irritability, and melancholy.

But our main focus will be on showing you how moving your body and eating high-value foods will increase the odds that you ride into your golden years with energy and vitality.

You don't need a background in anatomy or physiology to use this book. It simply weaves together information that we've learned over the course of our lives, and you can choose the tools presented here that work best for you.

The mind and body are fascinating subjects, but we haven't attempted to be comprehensive here. Rather, we focused on simple methods that have had an effect on our clients over the years. Different things work for different people, so choose the exercises and tips that work best for you.

A word of caution, please seek advice from a medical professional before you begin any new exercise regimen or diet.

Finally, if we know one thing for sure, it's that making small changes consistently will lead to big changes in your body and your experience of daily living.

Remember this, when you change your habits, you change your life.

If You Want to Live, Move! is an updated and simplified program that empowers you to take the right action each day on a consistent basis so you can realize the rich rewards that are rightfully yours – energy, strength, and renewed health.

This book is designed so that you can quickly access the nuts and bolts of our program and get right to it.

We have laid out this book to be an easy (and illuminating) read. If you need more information and motivation, we have included additional resources for that, as well.

Plus, we are here to help you every step of the way. Keep in touch with both of us at www.8minuteworkouts.com.

Let's take a closer look at how this book is organized.

The book is divided into three parts:

PART I – ReNew (The Right Mindset for Boomer success)

PART II – ReShape (The Move It section for Boomer success)

PART III – ReFuel (Eating as Fuel for Boomer success)

At the end of each chapter is a *Borrowed Wisdom for Boomers* section that details important inner guidance and wisdom from both Jaime and Elaine. We will also present some highlighted facts that you may find helpful.

Most importantly, we want you to let us know how you are doing. Won't you please take some time to email either of us at jaimebrenkus@gmail.com.

So, before we begin, let's take a few minutes to formally introduce ourselves.

ELAINE - The First Lady of Fitness

I am asked time and time again, "What is your secret to living a healthful, youthful life in your 90s?" My answer is simple, and I quote my late husband, Jack LaLanne. "Exercise is King. Nutrition is Queen. Put them together and you have a Kingdom."

My kingdom is exercising regularly, watching what food I put in my mouth, and making sure I am consistent about it.

When asked to team up with the designer of the *8-Minute Abs and Body* workouts, Jaime Brenkus, for this book, I knew we had the same philosophy. With all the talk and news coverage the boomers were getting regarding studies that found they were less fit than the last generation, Jaime, being a boomer, wanted to put the Boom back in the boomers. He approached my agent, Rick Hersh, with his idea and I was onboard, not only for the boomers but for anyone and everyone who will read this.

After all, exercise is exercise, food is food, and motivation is motivation. We are going to encourage you to incorporate movement into your daily life by following our 8-minute workouts, as well as making super easy food choices daily. We want to put the boom back in your life. Jack helped me, a former junk food junkie, put the boom back in my life, and Jaime and I want to share our knowledge with you. Keeping in shape is really easy when you know how! Are you ready? We are! So let's get started!

For more on the life of Jack and Elaine LaLanne, please turn to the back of this book.

JAIME - (Designer) of 8 Minute Abs series

I have been athletic all my life. Fortunately, staying in shape has come naturally to me. The first chance I had to help people with their fitness came in high school, where I was the team captain for our baseball team.

I was also given the responsibility to lead the team in our fitness regimen consisting of basic calisthenics, weight training, and sprints (this, by the way, was a predecessor of my future programming).

I loved that gratifying feeling of knowing I was making a difference in someone's life.

This carried over to my college days, where I coined my healthy lifestyle routine, which I called the 3-D system - *discipline, dedication, and determination.*

While my peers were out partying and carousing, I was getting up at 4:30 in the morning and hitting the gym, and then going to intern at Channel 8, an NBC affiliate in Tampa. I wanted to be a sports anchor, however, I had a vision of becoming a fitness star based on my knowledge of the subject, my drive, and my BS degree in Mass Communication. And I must admit, I had an affinity for being in front of the camera.

Jaime in his 20's

In 1985, after college, I moved to Los Angeles, joined a gym, and was discovered by a personal trainer there. He noticed my peculiar way of circuit training, where I would go from one machine to the other and intersperse jumping jacks and calisthenics between sets. I called this "Fitness Fusion" and later trademarked this routine for my franchise, Slim & Fit.

My trainer asked me to help one of his clients with his workout. Wow, I couldn't believe I was going to get paid for helping people get fit! That started my personal training career.

We joined forces for three years. However, I didn't want to be a little fish in a big pond, so I moved back to Tampa where I started my own fitness business and where I could expand my vision with products and TV fitness segments. The Tampa market was ripe for my programming, where I routinely appeared on TV and radio, and gained a following. I knew I needed a formal background to back up my fitness goals, so in 1988, I was certified as a Health Fitness Instructor from the American College of Sports Medicine.

Jaime in his 30's

It was there that I made a connection with a director who wanted to produce the *8 Minute Abs* videos series.

And from there, I am proud to share, we helped millions of people lose millions of pounds (and inches).

By producing videos, I could see that I could help more people at once than doing one-on-one training. So, I started to create fitness videos and I designed a popular one that resonated with a large number of people, called "8 Minute Abs". It was the first time anyone marketed an 8-minute video. It was different than the hour-long programs that were so popular until then.

It showed me that 'time' was a huge factor in people's lives, and I invested the time and energy in creating more programming based on the "minutes" element.

To date, the *8 Minute* series has had over 50 million views on YouTube!

The *8 Minute Abs* success opened the doors to realize other product lines and to choreograph supermodel Kathy Ireland's two top rated videos, *Body Specifics,* and *Reach.*

I knew that fitness was only one part of the lean equation, so with the help of a registered dietician from the Cleveland Clinic, we created a patented portion control plate that helped hundreds of thousands of people.

Jaime in his early 40's

Since my first video, I have now produced over 150 fitness video segments that can be completed in 5, 8, and 15 minutes intervals. My background in TV has allowed me to appear on various home shopping channels including QVC, HSN, Canadian Home Shopping and Value Vision.

A few years ago, I had the pleasure of appearing on the *Dr. Oz Show* as a fitness expert for the abs. Currently, I operate *Lean Living*, a fitness studio in Cleveland.

Jaime in his Late 50's

My body started to transform with the first nutrition course I took in college. I started to experiment with my body on what foods would produce the best results. I'm not 20 anymore, I'm in my late 50s, and people always ask me how I stay so lean for my age. I'm a creature of habits - good habits. I have developed a lean, toned, unintimidating, but attainable look. The timing is perfect for me to bring my knowledge to baby boomers.

Jaime in his late 50's living a lean lifestyle

The idea that I could craft a program for those of us who are boomers invigorated me.

I reached out to Jack Lalanne's wife, Elaine at their *BeFit* office in California, and as luck would have it, Elaine answered the phone, which is a rarity, she told me.

It's ironic that I'm writing a book with Elaine, since I owe plenty of what I've accomplished to her late husband, Jack.

I had a chance to meet Jack in 2001 in Chicago. I was introduced to Jack and Elaine from fitness pro, Denise Austin. She said "Hey Jack, this is Jaime. He's the *8 Minute Abs* guy."

Jack then proceeded to get me into a headlock and gave me a 'nuggie' on my head, laughing, "That's what's wrong with you guys. You only think there's one body part." We all had a nice chuckle. I was thrilled. I had finally met my fitness hero.

Jack's autograph photo hanging in Jaime's office

Through the years, I've watched fads come and go. And, as I get older, I'm seeing that what we did 40 and 50 years ago is still effective today.

I've dedicated my life to serving you. It's gratifying to me knowing that I'm able to help change your life. My sole purpose for going to work every morning is to help people live a healthier lifestyle. It is truly my passion to be able to assist you turn your desires into reality with a workable action plan.

Jaime in his late 50's, leading by example

Elaine, who appeared on Jack's show, is in her 90s and can still do a full body push up. Imagine that! She must know something. Elaine is truly a walking billboard for health!

Whatever your motivation to change might be – make no mistake - you're in good hands with Elaine and me. Thank you so much for entrusting us with your health and body. Together, we'll make sure that you succeed and live a more vibrant lifestyle.

I want to congratulate you for taking the first step towards a healthy, new you.

Jaime

PART ONE: RENEW

"If you are going to conquer the force within you that is holding you back from being fit. First, you must have the desire, the goal in mind, and believe with every fiber of your being you can conquer, because you are, not only what you eat, but what you think! Above all, you are responsible for your health and if you are not willing to be honest with you, believe in you, and develop a new set of rules for living, you will fizzle out and waste away."

Jack LaLanne

Chapter 1: BOOMERS. Begin Anew

"The best time to plant a tree was 20 years ago. The second-best time is now."

Chinese proverb

Maybe you haven't yet planted that seed. You've been busy. You've had other more important matters to tend to. (Hopefully, in reading this book, we can convince you that taking care of your body is *the* most important matter to tend to.)

What's essential is that you take advantage of the time you have NOW.

What if we could help you find the time, starting with only 8 minutes, to begin your journey of a total mind, body and spiritual transformation, no matter where you are in your life?

You don't need to wait for everything to be perfect in your life before you make a change for the better. In fact, if we all did that, we would be waiting forever. Now is the perfect time to decide to improve your health so you can avoid and reduce chronic disease and pain and improve your mobility, stamina, range of motion, your energy, and your zest for life.

Bring Back your Boom

Our primary reason for writing this book for you is to prove that with just a little bit of time moving your body (8 minutes to start) and a commitment to eating healthy, you can help yourself to a brand-new life.

If you have dreamed of reshaping your body and creating a turning point in your life where you are deeply satisfied with who is staring back at you in the mirror, we're here to help you do just that. Our goal is to put the boom back into your step and life.

We want this book to ignite you, engage you and empower you. Whether you're a busy professional, trying to balance work and a personal life, or you are an exhausted, overscheduled parent or grandparent, we can assure you the days of yo-yo diets, restricted eating, and all or nothing exercise programs are in your rearview mirror.

Do you find yourself saying you would love to get started on a program very soon, but that moment never arrives? We're all guilty of procrastination, and to overcome this mindset, Elaine's late husband, Jack, would always come back to these two words, *Pride* and *Discipline*, which he defined further as taking pride in yourself and having the discipline to continually stay in shape.

There is never a perfect time to start eating healthier or start an exercise program. It's always tomorrow, next week, next month or never. The time to take action is now. Out of the 1,440 minutes in the day, isn't it wise to invest 8 minutes in you?

We ask that you don't look backward or forward. Each daily victory is all that counts. By living in the moment today, you will gain the 'motivation traction' to make tomorrow even better.

Plant the seed, water it, **with small goals,** and watch it grow.

When possible, visualize what the new you will look like. Keep that vision in your mind as you go about your daily life.

Make no mistake, this lifestyle prescription isn't about will power, as you already have it. After all, didn't you will your-self to get up this morning, brush your teeth and get dressed? It takes WANT power! You have to WANT to be healthier and stronger. You have to WANT more energy, WANT more vitality and WANT more self-confidence.

We can assure you your personal pride will flourish with each circuit of exercise you perform, each healthy meal you eat, and each daily victory you accomplish. These little things you change today will change the rest of your life.

Back to the Basics

Before we take the first step, let's reflect on how we view our bodies. Often, we judge ourselves too harshly (fat, thin, tall, short, ugly, old, etc.), but if you pause to dig deeper, you begin to realize a few fundamental truths.

Your body is in flux, constantly changing. Not only physically, but in the form of thoughts and emotions.

Everything you do, every thought and emotion you have, impacts you on a physiological level, causing a chain reaction.

When you begin to view your body as a dynamic living force, you begin to see how change is possible with one new thought, which can lead to one new action, which will open the door to a powerful transformation. (Bottom line: what we think changes how we act.)

Two tenets which will support your healthy transformation are movement and diet, along with a good night's sleep.

Move

We titled this book after one of Jack's most famous quotes, "If you want to live, move." The most important thing is to get creative with the ways in which you move; take a walk in the park, walk your dog, stroll the baby, clean your house, swim in a pool or lake.

Throughout this book, we will talk about exercise as a way of movement. But if you take nothing else from this book, remember this: Move and move often, with joy and enthusiasm.

Diet

There are many ideas and theories on diets. Simply put, eat your food in the right amount; food that doesn't come in a box or a can. Jack said over and over again, "If man made it, don't eat it."Eat vegetables, fruits, nuts and seeds, meats, eggs and fish. Shop at your local farmers market and make every effort to avoid processed food.

Borrowed Wisdom: On Attitude Adjustment

I think Maya Angelou hit Attitude right on the head by her quote, "If you don't like something change it. If you can't change it then change your attitude!" A number of years ago, we received a letter from a viewer who felt she had hit rock bottom. Her favorite uncle died, not only her car but the roof on her house needed major repairs, just one thing after the other including the fact that she thought her friends had let her down. She was sad, miserable and constantly complained, and blamed her problems on others. As she tells it, "I made everyone else miserable then I heard you, Jack, talking about attitudes and that you can change bad ones for good ones. I took a look into myself and decided I just had to deal with everything. When I changed my attitude, my whole life changed around."

Think about people you know who have a negative attitude and note how they act and what they say. Do you want to be around them? Now, think about people you know that are always positive and happy; personally, those are the people I want to be around.

I've learned that having a positive outlook can make all the difference in your life. Remember, every entrance has an exit and if you entered into a negative attitude you can always exit and enter into a positive one.

~Elaine

"If you are around "LaLa" for any length of time, you'll find that her enthusiasm for life is contagious. She can do pushups, chin ups; she's a terrific golfer, and swimmer. She is a lecturer, author, civic leader, and business woman; a super wife and good friend. To me she is living proof of all that a woman should be."

Jack LaLanne

Chapter 2: BOOMERS. Defined

Technically speaking, a baby boomer is defined as a person born between 1946 and 1964. The boomer demographic cohort is sandwiched between the *Silent Generation* and the *Millennials*.

As of 2016, the number of baby boomers ranged from 74.1 million to 81.3 million, depending on whether the generation began with the birth year 1943 or 1946.

As a group, baby boomers are debatably the wealthiest, most active, and most physically fit generation to enter this world (once upon a time...).

As they grew older, they joined the fitness revolution and became physically fit. However, as time marched on, career, procrastination, and many excuses got in the way. Consequently, they find themselves now having to fight the "Battle of the Bulges".

If you can relate, it's never too late. THE TIME IS NOW TO GET IN SHAPE!

Jack LaLanne and the Modernization of Fitness

Elaine's late husband, Jack LaLanne, lauded as "The God-father of Modern Fitness," and the founder of the modern physical fitness movement, clearly has something to do with the way the fitness revolution began.

Jack enthusiastically ushered boomers into what was considered by many to be the golden era of health. He helped change the popular idea that exercise would make you muscle bound.

LaLanne reached millions of viewers through *The Jack LaLanne Show,* which debuted decades before Jane Fonda and Richard Simmons ever arrived on the health and fitness scene. His intimacy with his audience was arguably his greatest appeal.

He would do a trick by blowing up his bicep muscle, have his dog, Happy, say his prayers, and roll over or jump over Jack's outstretched leg. Jack also made sure he told the boomers to go get mommy and daddy or whoever was in the house that, "Jack is waiting for them to come and exercise."

Boomers were the generation that put "fitness" on the map. They were no strangers to throwing frisbees on the beach, pumping iron at the gym, riding their bicycles across the hills and valleys of their hometowns.

Boomers didn't take no for an answer and expected life to deliver to them in grand fashion everything they asked of it.

They moved their bodies and created movements. (Civil rights, anti-war, women's rights, and environmental causes were the reasons they marched across the map.)

They were not old enough to remember any personal details of WWII, but old enough to secure the profits of a post war era.

But, lest we forget, boomers had their own wars to deal with. Staging protests against the Vietnam War, fighting in it; or dodgers and deserters, catching trains and buses to Canada.

Boomers were a generation of Coca-Cola and Beatlemania, Rock n' Roll and Motown, many who grew up watching *The Brady Bunch, Batman, Johnny Carson* and *The Ed Sullivan Show.*

(And as mentioned, The Jack LaLanne Show.*)*

Boomers sat in their living rooms, watching the news unfold on their black and white televisions covering unforgettable events such as the Cold War, the Cuban Missile Crisis, the assassinations of JFK, Robert Kennedy and MLK Jr.

It wasn't all gloom and doom, however; America was a prospering nation. And to prove the undeniable power of the United States of America, President Kennedy set out to show the world we could fly man to the moon and bring him safely back to earth.

On July 20, 1969, televised broadcasts confirmed it to be true. Outside the Apollo 11 lunar module, standing on the moon's ancient cratered surface, in front of the camera held by moon wayfarer astronaut Buzz Aldrin, Astronaut Neil Armstrong delivered these eleven immortal words:

"That's one small step for man, one giant leap for mankind."

America was on the map.

A revolution of sorts had begun.

Fitness in America Then

In December 1960, President-elect John F. Kennedy wrote an open letter to the public addressing his concerns about the declining fitness of the U.S. population. The essay was published in *Sports Illustrated* magazine.

In this cover story titled *"The Soft American,"* Kennedy expressed his concern that the lack of "physical vigor" could possibly put the nation in a position of being unable to defend itself during war or prosper during peacetime.

"Physical fitness is the basis of all the activities of our society," Kennedy wrote. "And if our bodies grow soft and inactive, if we fail to encourage physical development and prowess, we will undermine our capacity for thought, for work and for the use of those skills vital to an expanding and complex America."

In 1966 (exactly 30 years after Jack opened the first modern health spa - which would later become the mega gym *Bally's*) President Lyndon Johnson established the first *Presidential Physical Fitness Awards*.

And then, in the 90s, the game changer led by Fonda's "feel the burn" and Richard Simmons' "love yourself for all of you" moves.

In 1995, Jaime came onto the scene as Americans became more time conscious and abs conscious, eventually reaching runaway success with *8 Minute Abs* videos, helping millions of people achieve a slimmer, trimmer, tighter waistline.

Fitness in America Now

Then the unpredictable happened.

Boomers, once the most physically fit generation, went from fit to flabby almost overnight.

This was an interesting turn of events since surveys show boomers are concerned about many aspects of their future. Looking for ways to cut their daily living expenses, studies show they are shopping for healthier foods, working out to stay fit, and looking for ways to control the cost of their healthcare.

According to the *Centers for Disease Control and Prevention,* over 36% of adults in the United States age 60 or older are obese. This number is expected to rise as the baby boomer generation ages. It's estimated 32 percent of older adults get no physical exercise whatsoever.

That's why we want you to reshape.

Borrowed Wisdom: On Visualization

I became aware and started to look back on my life and it dawned on me that I actually visualized my career in television when, in 1949, television was in its infancy. I was sitting in my living room with a brand new, small, black and white television and picturing myself on it. At that time, I was demonstrating RCA 45 record players at department stores in San Francisco. One fateful day I was scheduled to demonstrate at the Emporium Department store where Les Malloy, a famous disc jockey, was making a personal appearance. He overheard me pitching the RCA 45 Record player to all who would listen. Maybe what caught his attention was when I answered a customer, "No you can't get Bing Crosby," who was on competitor, Columbia 33/1/3 Records, "but you can get Perry Como and he sounds just like him." He asked me if I would be interested in doing a show with him on Television and can I have a show ready by next Tuesday and he would give me leads to get guests for the 90 minute interview TV show. I took one gulp and said yes!!!! If I hadn't said yes, I would never met my husband Jack LaLanne. My visual picture paid off.

In all of Jack's famous swimming feats he would say to me "I always visualize myself coming out of the water, even when he got caught in the pilings on one of his swims from Alcatraz, handcuffed, feet shackled and towing a 1000 pound boat, he didn't give up, he kept seeing himself coming out of the water, mission accomplished!" He visualized all the equipment he invented such as the wall pulleys, the leg extension machine, the squat machine and the first weight selector. His visualization, believing, being positive, and a having sense of humor was a key part of his life. Jack was always positive. I don't think he knew the word negative. I don't think a day ever went by without hearing him say, "Anything in life is possible and you can make it happen." I called it his "mantra" whether he was signing autographs, lecturing, talking to strangers, to me, or his family.

~Elaine

Still looking young on a TV set...Elaine 60, and Jack 71 years old.

PART TWO: RESHAPE

Chapter 3: Boomers. Moving Your Body

According to guidelines set by the American College of Sports Medicine, *Physical Activity Guidelines for Americans*, you need to do two types of physical activity each week to improve your health - aerobic and muscle-strength training.

Adults need moderate-intensity aerobic activity (brisk walking) every week and muscle-strength activities two or more days a week (those that hit all major muscle groups: legs, arms, chest, back, shoulders, abs).

Adults' exercise needs differ from younger people because of their metabolism (the rate at which a person burns energy). Mother Nature has a way of turning down our body's metabolism. Because research shows that every decade starting at the age of 25, our metabolism declines. Additionally, when you exercise in your 50s, 60s, and 70s you don't burn as many calories as you did during your younger years.

Our exercise and diet regimen are adjusted as we age, therefore, it's even more important to follow a healthy lifestyle.

You must come up with your own reasons for coming on board the boomer train. Any reason is a good reason, as long as it's yours. It might be to lose weight, to gain strength, to lower your risk of disease or improve your mood, or it may simply be you are sick and tired of being sick and tired.

Fortunately, we don't have to wait to make changes for the better and to create a turning point in our lives.

You may look at this information, and see your time being devoured. But, stay with us and we will show you how a little here and a little there will offer A LOT over time.

You have the power to change. Right this very minute.

There has been a fast-growing body of evidence in the last several years that lack of exercise – or sedentariness – is a major risk factor in health. It's been linked to heart disease, cancer, and to an early death.

A recent study by the *American Journal of Clinical Nutrition* finds that lack of exercise may actually be even **more** of a risk than obesity in early mortality.

Lack of exercise may actually be even more of a risk than obesity in early mortality! If you Rest, you Rust!

Research shows, exercise can extend your life, no matter how inactive you are now.

Tufts John Hancock Research Center on Physical Activity Nutrition and Obesity Prevention, Miram E. Nelson, PhD says "it doesn't take a lot to make a major difference."

Exercise can extend your life and the greatest benefits come from just getting started. Nelson further asserts, "The less active you are now, the more benefit you get from adding even a small amount of exercise to your life."

Along with regular exercise, the next step is to adjust your eating habits. Because exercise and nutrition are intimately connected – which we get into later – stay tuned.

Borrowed Wisdom: On Positive Self Talk

We like to call it Negative Mind Enemy. (NME = Enemy) Negative thought patterns can lead you in a downward spiral, and contribute to self-criticism, self-blame, and negative expectations. NME happens to all of us. We have to create positive self-talk language and redirect ourselves when the negative exchange happens. Negative thinking tends to erode our ability to progress.

~Jaime

Your brain needs exercise too. Exercise helps improve memory problems. According to the American Medical Association (AMA), "Exercise improves cognitive [memory] function in older adults with subjective and objective mild cognitive impairment. The benefits of physical activity were

When you begin your healthy weight management routine, remember that the main goal is to get in shape and to stay fit, not necessarily to drop a major amount of weight all at once.

And, it is NOT TOO LATE to kick into gear.

You have leaves blowing in your flower beds? Rake them. You have a grandbaby you can stroll in the stroller? Stroll him. If you have a partner you can walk a couple blocks (or miles) with? Walk with them.

apparent after 6 months and persisted for at least another 12 months after [our study] had been discontinued."

"Reverse the aging process, one step at a time."

Elaine LaLanne

If you have been away from strength training for a long time, or a beginner, you can begin to reap the benefits at any age. The sooner you start, the better your chances of building and maintaining benefits that will last a lifetime.

The benefits of strength training are there for your choosing; but, you must be committed to the process towards better health. You must change your lifestyle.

Once you stop weight training, or any form of exercise, your body will adapt to that lack of demand. The result? Weakness and the downward-spiral effect called muscle atrophy.

Muscle Loss in Boomers

FIX YOUR FLABBY-SEAT-IT IS: As we age, we tend to lose muscle, and muscle loss creates weakness. Resistance training, body weight exercises, and sufficient protein intake help to put the brakes on this progression.

Far too often we witness someone aging, sometimes many years before their time. They become less active for any number of reasons or excuses.

Many of us (wrongly) think this is a normal part of aging. We speed up the aging process when we stop moving. Our bodies were designed to work and move.

You can learn to do some exercises and take back your power.

It's your choice!

32

Borrowed Wisdom: On Perfection

I always suggest to my clients that they aim for progress over perfection.

What do I mean by that? Let me illustrate with an example.

I have seen far too many people give up on themselves because they simply couldn't see how much progress they had made toward their goal(s). When a client is tempted to throw in the towel too early, I always try to encourage otherwise. I do this by reminding clients (over and over again, if necessary) that our aim is not 100% perfection, rather it is 100% progress. Progress is a given if a client is taking the action steps.

I worked with one client who had lost 2 pants sizes over a period of just 8 weeks. She was clearly making progress. However, her goal was to develop a perfect body, like one of those beautiful models on the cover of a magazine. This became her sole obsession, and each time she was working out she would comment, "I'm not there yet." She didn't take the time to notice that she was, in fact, in the process of transformation, which is to say, she WAS transforming. But, in her mind, she still didn't meet this idea of perfection.

And despite her transformation (she had lost inches), she convinced herself she was failing, and in less than a three-month period, she quit when she could have simply redirected herself. Her NME (Negative Mind Enemy) won! Don't let that happen to you. Focus on your progress.

Being negative can also destroy your self-confidence and send your self-esteem into a free fall, making it hard for you to feel good about yourself. This frustration leads to a downward spiral of disappointment and disillusionment which can cause you to feel inadequate in many parts of your life.

People take varied routes to reach the same goal, so find the pace at which you feel comfortable and proceed from there. We'll be giving you one or two new skills to implement every day. Keep in mind that some skills take more time to master than others.

For instance, it may take some people a while to learn how to shop efficiently, yet for others it may take only one trip to the grocery store. Whatever your rate of change, please be patient. Changing any habit takes time, determination, discipline, confidence, sacrifice and commitment. We're not telling you it's going to be easy, we're telling you it's going to be worth it!

~Jaime

Today is a fine day to start your journey on your path to better health. If you wish for a longer, independent, more comfortable, and productive life – to put the boom back in it – we are behind you 100 percent!

Boomer Facts

- The loss of strength and stamina attributed to aging is in part caused by reduced physical activity.

- Inactivity increases with age. By age 75, about one in three men and one in two women engage in no physical activity.

- Among adults aged 65 years and older, walking and gardening or yard work are, by far, the most popular physical activities.

- Social support from family and friends has been consistently and positively related to regular physical activity.

- Exercise has countless benefits for those of all ages, including a healthier heart, stronger bones and improved flexibility. For seniors, there are additional benefits, like the fact that regular exercise reduces the risk of chronic diseases, lowers the chance of injury and can even improve one's mood.

- As we age, our muscle mass begins to decrease. When we enter our forties, adults can lose 3-5% of muscle mass with each subsequent decade of life. Muscle is an essential contributor to our balance and bone strength; it keeps us strong. Without it, our mobility and independence become compromised.

- Exercise is also a key for cognitive function. Scientists have found that brain neurons - the special cells that perform all the necessary function to keep you alive, as well as help you think and improve your memory- all increase after a few weeks of regular exercise. In fact, some researchers found that when individuals walk three or more times a week, the occurrence of dementia was 35% lower than those seniors who were not involved in any type of physical activity.

- Regular exercise by seniors may decrease the time it takes for a wound to heal by 25%. Also, a healthy, strong body can better fight off infection and makes recovery from illness or injury easier.

"When you build or tear down a house you need different kinds of tools, right? What is so different about building or tearing down your body, you also need various tools but dissimilar ones. Those dissimilar ones are the tools we are referring to, to help you build your body into what you desire."

Elaine LaLanne

Fitness is cumulative! A little here, a little there. Based on long-term data, *The American College of Sports Medicine,* and other governing fitness bodies and experts, found that you can gain benefits by doing shorter bouts of fitness. And, any movement **that lasted longer than 5 minutes** is considered a bout of exercise!

"He who has no Time for his Health today will have no Health for his Time tomorrow!"

Jaime Brenkus

8 Minutes at a Time

We are sure that you can find 8 minutes somewhere during the day.

Let's do the math. In a 24-hour period, you have exactly 180 of those 8 minute segments. Can you justify spending *one* of those segments on your health?

And can you see that you will still have 179 segments left to accomplish so much more?

By engaging in an 8 minute a day regimen, you build a consistent habit of doing some sort of fitness activity. 8 minutes will establish a positive habit you can build on.

Of course, we want to be perfectly frank here. The ultimate goal is to turn those 8 minutes into 16, and 16 into 24, and so on.

Be Grateful and Happy

Be grateful for your wonderfully made body. You have eyes to see, a nose to breathe, a mouth and digestive system to eat and eliminate, arms and hands to hug and lift, legs to walk and run, and feet to stand. We are truly fearfully and wonderfully made. However, we need to keep that body in perfectly running order like we do our cars. We must oil our joints with movement and wholesome food. If you are embarking on a journey to reshape and renew your body, you may want to start with your mind.

Keep a daily a log of your negative thoughts, then replace them with a positive one.

You'll hear this more than once, that, "thoughts are things!" Writing down your negative thoughts is a way of helping you snap out of denial to get moving. If you are content with a life of no exercise and poor nutrition then ask yourself, "What is the prognosis of my health in the next 10 years?" Time flits by pretty fast the older you get, and what are you going to look and feel like then? Be grateful that it is never too late to begin to change. If you are having trouble getting motivated and you are not moved by the research that *If you Want to Live, Move* presents, here is a little story that Jack wrote, years ago, in his book, *Revitalize Your Life,* that might give you some incentive.

The Story of Ike & Mike

Once upon a time there were two middle aged frogs, Ike and Mike, who lived upon a grassy knoll above some deep tractor tracks on a farm. Although he was overweight, Ike was contented, loved to snare as many flies as he could, and wasn't much for jumping around. On the other hand, Mike loved to jump and eat his flies sparingly, often jumping in and out of the deep tractor tracks. Both spent their days croaking happily. Mike and Ike had it made and they knew it. One day while reaching for a fly, Ike lost his balance and landed in the deep tractor rut with a loud *Hummmph!* There he remained unable to leap back up to his grassy knoll.

Mike kept yelling, "Jump out, jump out!" Ike forlornly shook his head and cried, "I can't, I can't, I'm just too old and too heavy, I'm over the hill!" Suddenly he heard a rumbling and looking back a big farm tracker was rolling down the road ready to crush Ike to death, the closer the tracker came Ike tried to leap out but just couldn't move. "Is this," he thought, "my end? And so young." Croaking in terror as the tractor came closer, he had to do something. He gave one last tremendous leap and landed safely on the knoll. It happened so suddenly it amazed even him. He had lifted himself out of the rut. Mike was cheering loudly, saying, "You did it, Ike, you did it! How in the world did you do it?" Ike answered, "I HAD TO!"

There are many kinds of ruts in our life and many ways of falling into them, but there is always a way to get out. Most ruts are a state of mind and getting out doesn't always require desperation leaps. The first step is to change your thinking. If you're in a rut, don't accept it. Learn to fight for your life. The rest of your life is the best of your life.

"If you are in a rut and out of condition forgive yourself and start over."

Elaine

Borrowed Wisdom: On Forgiving

One thing among the many others I've learned, is that I had to learn to not only forgive others, but to forgive myself. As I look back, I've made many stupid decisions, but I have made good ones, too.

Now if I keep thinking of the stupid ones, where is it getting me? Only thinking of more stupid ones and making me miserable. Only to go backward instead of forward. Now if I concentrate on the good ones, it gives me self-assurance and that I can make more good decisions, and it helps to give me an optimistic outlook for the future.

As a child, I was shy and afraid to speak up because I thought my opinion would not be pertinent, nor would it be as smart and knowledgeable as others. Through the years, I finally know who I am, and I have learned that I do have something to say. Once you see yourself in the spectrum you can see and understand others better.

~Elaine

Chapter 4: BOOMERS. Time is on Your Side

Before we get into the nitty-gritty of your new regimen, here's a suggestion for finding time for your 8-minute workouts. Write down on a piece of paper and divide your day into three parts:

- Waking up through Lunch

- End of Lunch to Dinner

- End of Dinner until you go to sleep

How do you fill up these hours of your day? For instance, you may spend 30 minutes getting ready for work, 20 minutes eating breakfast, having your coffee and reading the paper. How many minutes do you spend talking on the phone? Shopping? Cooking? Taking naps? Watching TV? Socializing? Daydreaming?

You will be able to see patterns in your lifestyle on how your valuable time is spent. There have to be 8 minutes that you can spare.

Daily Victories

Don't look backward - only look forward to what you visualize as the end result. You are not living in yesterday, nor are you living in tomorrow. This moment is the only moment you're living in. This is the time to plant your seed and begin your remodeling. If you start today with just a few minutes of exercise, it is a victory. Look forward to each daily victory.

Your life is divided into 24 separate 60-minute vignettes every day. How you choose to divide your "portions" will affect every part of who you are.

Remember, the process of change happens day by day, month by month - the more you do, the more you can do, and then it becomes a habit. If you have this moment to start to do a little movement, and then a little bit more, it accumulates, like putting money in a bank. The more you put in, the more you can take out. And then it becomes a habit in your life. Now that's a daily victory.

With this approach, you will not fail. No goal is ever achieved until it finds its way into your daily thoughts and actions. Then it becomes a part of you. The little things that you can change TODAY - will change your life, without turning your life upside down**!**

Borrowed Wisdom: On Negative Statements

Stay away from hurtful phrases like:

*I can't do this, it's not going to work
I won't stick with it, I never do*

There's no way, it's too hard
I'm too fat
I hate my thighs
I have a big butt
I don't have any willpower

Negative statements to ourselves usually stop our action plans,
so we normally don't move forward with our positive, lean habits.
We need to make a conscious effort to STOP it - before it STOPS
you. Plant the seed to succeed!

I'm full of energy today
I feel I'm taking good care of myself
I am really proud of myself for eating well
I am following my doctor's advice

~Jaime

Watch your 'Negative' Language

We've learned by working with all body types and all ages that most people choose to see the negative aspects about themselves, rather than the positive, especially when it comes to their bodies. This only demolishes your chances for success if you are prone to negative thoughts about yourself. First, be honest. Take a close look at your thoughts and see if you can identify what elements are playing a role in your battle with your body. You have the power, and can change and transform, creating a healthy lifestyle NOW! That is, if you choose to. It's all up to you!!

We're confident that when you have built a positive habit of engaging your body in fitness, you are 100% more likely to make time in your busy schedule to continue this habit.

YOU are the priority! Like anything else, we make time for things that are a priority for us.

Make it a priority to wake up a few minutes earlier in the morning, hop off the sofa during the commercial breaks of your favorite TV show for a few arm exercises. Or, squeeze your exercise into a coffee break at work. In other words, you will Find Time!

There's always time to make moving your body a priority.

Before you begin, here are a few quick tips.

Borrowed Wisdom: On Rehashing the Past (I USTA)

I've learned not to take the time to rehash over something that has already happened. Jack had a sign made for our house which I have in the kitchen. "Yesterday has gone, tomorrow isn't here yet, so today is the most important day of your life". If you keep reliving the past, you live in the past and you can't move forward. I can still hear him saying, "Don't be a 'Usta'...I 'usta' workout, I 'usta' be in good shape, but I'm too old to get it back."

I usta be able to do 25 pushups but...but, but what? I have learned that I cannot change the present, I have to accept what comes and take the bitter with the sweet.

~Elaine

Chapter 5: BOOMERS. A Selfie and a Tape Measure

The first and the most important step in tracking your fitness progress is take a picture of yourself every 4-6 weeks. This will help you in tracking if your body is transitioning in the right direction. It's motivating seeing your progress, not to mention your new wardrobe.

Number ONE: It's important to take your body measurements. Even if you're not losing pounds, you will be losing inches all over your body as your figure "leans out" and firms up with muscles. Measuring your body tends to be more reliable than the scale. We're not asking you to get rid of your scale, but to be more mindful of what the tape measure reveals. It's not about the number, it's about the SIZE.

Below is a chart that shows you where and how to take your measurements.

This is the starting point on your journey to a healthier, more energetic you!

Tape your BEFORE photo here for EXTRA INSPIRATION!

Let's Measure!

Step 1:

Choose a "before" snapshot to paste into the space above, because we want you to remember where you started. Days, weeks, and a few short months from now, you'll be amazed at how far you've come.

Step 2:

You'll need a measuring tape for this next part. Take your measurements and record them in your personal chart. We recommend you measure no more than once a month, but at least once each month.

Step 3:

We've also provided spaces for clothing sizes. You may find that you have dropped a size, so we want you to have space for recording your progress when you do buy something.

You'll be amazed at where you lose inches when you lose weight. Often, watch bands and rings need adjustments. Some people's shoe size even gets smaller.

Be sure you measure accurately the same way each time you measure your progress. Don't pull the tape too tight! Skin should not "bulge" at the edges of the tape. Standing in front of a full-length mirror when you measure can be helpful for more accurate results.

Don't throw your scale away, we've provided a spot for your weight.

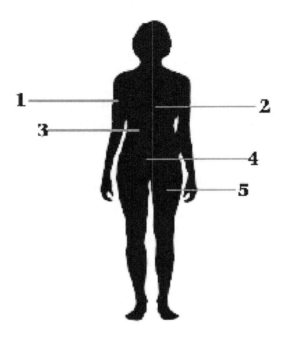

1. Upper Arm: the widest part of the biceps, only one arm

2. Bust/Chest: the widest part, across the nipples

3. Waist: midway between the bust/chest and the hips

4. Hips: the widest part of the buttock, feet together

5. Thigh-single: the widest part of the thigh

MEASUREMENT/WEIGHT/CLOTHING SIZE PROGRESS CHART (FILL IN AND DRAW BELOW)						
MEASUREMENT	START	WEEK 4	WEEK 8	WEEK 16	WEEK 20	TOTAL LOSS
Upper Arm						
Bust/Chest						
Waist						
Hips						
Thigh - Left						
Thigh - Right						
WEIGHT						
SIZES						
Tops						
Pants						
Skirts						
Dresses						
Jackets/Coats						
Underwear						
Bras						
Pantyhose						
Shoes						
Ring						

Now that you've taken your measurements, and before we get into your remodeling, we want you to realize this is what's going to happen to you….

Afterburn Effect

There's a scientific term called Excess Post-exercise Oxygen Consumption, (EPOC). It's the afterburn effect, which can help you burn more calories long after you've worked out. This is pure physics. When your muscles are stressed and stimulated, they grow and get stronger and the result is that they burn more calories at rest.

With our program, your afterburn increases as a result of the constant movement and intensity of not resting in between exercises. Result: Your energy has to return to its resting state which causes you to burn calories even AFTER your workout is over. Remember, this is what Jack was referring to in his quote, "Your Health Account is Like Your Bank Account."

The magic of strength training in achieving a healthy body, is that you can burn calories not only while you exercise, but also after you exercise.

Lean people get lean this way, stay lean and put on more muscle. Use your scale sparingly, to see if you're on an even keel, your *SIZE* matters. You'll be losing inches while you're firming and toning, but the scale may not budge because of all those defined, sculpted muscles you're now wearing. Only 8 minutes can start to change your life!

How to choose your weights

When you first start working out it's confusing what to do regarding the proper workload, whether it be in a gym or at home. "How much weight should I use?" is a valid question for someone just starting. You never want to hurt yourself working out – nor should you if you follow these basic guidelines.

It's important to choose a weight that you're comfortable with, and that you can safely lift 10 -15 times for each exercise. Also choose one where you can get the proper workload. If you choose a weight that you can only lift 3 or 4 times – that's too heavy – you need to go lighter. On the other hand, if you can lift a weight 25 times, that's way too light – and it's not enough for the muscle to grow or what we call hypertrophy.

As we age, and don't exercise, our lung capacity tends to shrink, and it becomes harder to breathe. Our exercises will help keep the lungs open. Here's a simple way to gauge your exertion level:

Take the Talk test

While you're exercising, if you're gasping for air, you're working way too hard and need to slow it down.

If you can recite the Gettysburg Address without missing a beat, then you probably need to pick up the pace. However, if you can hold a normal conversation, then that's about right. Keep up this steady state of conditioning and celebrate getting fit.

Heart Rate Check

When you are working out, be sure to check with your doctor or health professional for any reason you shouldn't be training. When you are beginning it is important to not overdo. As Jack said, "Make Haste Slowly" and the Mayo Clinic says "build intensity gradually." We agree! Many people like to take their Heart Rate to see if they are working in a safe range.

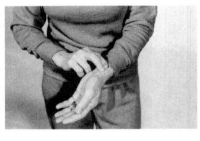

If you don't have access to a wearable tech device which measures your heart rate (and a bunch of other cool things), taking your pulse is a relatively simple matter. You can take your pulse rate at either the neck or the wrist. The radial pulse (wrist) is located on the underside of the wrist, in the little hollow on the thumb side. Don't take your pulse with your thumb (it has its own beat). Turn your right or left hand, palm up, and gently but firmly place your first two fingers over the pulse point. When you feel it beating, count the pulse for 15 seconds and multiply by four, or count to 30 seconds and multiply by two to get your resting pulse rate.

If you're going to engage in an intense workout, and you want to see if you're in a safe range, the chart below will help you stay in that range.

Here is how you find your target Heart Rate while working out. Start with the number 220, subtract your age, and that is your maximum pulse rate. Now to see if you're in your target zone, your base training pulse rate is 60 to 80% of your maximum heart rate. For example: If you're 50 years old subtract that from 220 and that gives you 170 as your maximum heart rate. Now take 60% of the 170 and you have your minimum target range which is 102. If you took 80%, it would be 136 beats per minute. You often see people who are running or cycling putting their fingers up to their neck and taking their pulse to see if they're in their target zone.

Elaine Checking Her Pulse

Age	60% of Maximum Heart Rate	80% of Maximum Heart Rate
20	120	160
25	117	156
30	114	152
35	111	148
40	108	144
45	105	140
50	102	136
55	99	132
60	96	128
65	93	124
70	90	120

Heart Rate Chart

Our approach to fitness is sensible and painless. You don't have to be a bodybuilder, or a marathon runner to see results.

Most people have busy schedules and share the same goals. They want to lose weight, inches, and, firm and tone their bodies. We're here to tell you that if you can work out with us 8 minutes every day, that's almost an hour a week, not an hour a day – and it's a great start. Remember, you don't have to torture your body in order for your body to respond.

Be Consistent

We want you to combine resistance and constant movement in the same workout, which will yield the best long-term, optimum results, in the shortest amount of time.

54

Rethink Your Definition of Exercise

If you're truly strapped for time, rethink your definition of exercise. We often get stuck in the trap of thinking that exercise means running or walking 3 miles or working out for hours. However, that's not the only way to think about exercise, think about 8 minutes a day. So, if you're busy, and who isn't? Don't let lack of time be your excuse. There is always something you can do, even if it's a little bit at a time. Eight minutes goes a long way. To quote Jack, "Something is better than nothing!"

Fitness RX

One question we are often asked is how one progresses on a program like this. Very simply, it's predicated on the amount of exertion you are putting forth or it's the amount of weight you're lifting that will dictate your progression. So, the more effort you put forth comes out in your vim, vigor and vitality.

So, the saying, "It never gets easier, you only get stronger," is true. Are you ready to take action?

Routine to Lean

These quick, consistent moves set you up to start your day on the right note, realizing that you've already accomplished a healthy habit for yourself early in the morning.

"People don't die of old age, they die of inactivity."

Jack LaLanne

Borrowed Wisdom: On Negative Thinking

My negative mind awakening happened years ago when I was playing in a closely contested golf tournament. My shot to the green landed on the right side of the sand trap, which meant I had go over the deep sand trap to land my ball on the green, hopefully near the pin. My first thought was, "I could lose this tournament if I go in the trap." Oops! This was a case of Negative Mind Energy! My ball not only went into the trap, but I missed the next shot out of the sand.

Needless to say, I lost the tournament, but I discovered something about my thinking patterns. I had heard and was aware that thoughts were 'things' but my brain didn't recognize this. So, the next time I played golf I tested myself. When I believed I could get over a water hole, I could. When I thought I couldn't, I missed, and the ball sunk in the water.

This example that our words and our thoughts can become 'things' has stayed with me all my life and I have trained my brain to be positive and eliminate the negative. Whether you're in a golf game or the game of life, negative thinking can either make you or break you!

~Elaine

Chapter 6: BOOMERS. Early Morning Secrets of Jaime and Elaine

C ore & More. When one thinks of core, often the first thing that comes to mind is the core of the apple. Core is the nucleus, the tough part of something that holds it together. Our core consists of the muscles around our trunk and pelvis. Core exercises train the muscles in your pelvis, lower back, hips and abdomen to work in harmony so that they can become strong and stable. Strong core muscles make it easier to do functional activities such as golf, get an object from a top shelf or even tie your shoes. Weak core muscles can lead to fatigue, less endurance and injuries. Strengthening core muscles may also help improve back pain. So, lets get started with some early morning exercises.

Elaine's Magic 5 Wake up exercises:

The Morning 5

Start with these 5 moves:

1. Knees to chest: Grab both knees and bring them up to your chest. Hold for 15 seconds.

2. Bicycle the legs: One of Jack's favorites... do this for 15 seconds.

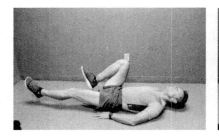 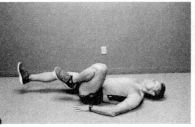

3. Hamstring stretch: Keep your leg straight and at 90 degrees, and gently pull your leg towards you. Hold for a count of 10 each leg.

4. Twisters: Keep one leg straight down on bed-while you place your opposite leg gently across and over the straight leg. Do 2 each side.

5. Criss-cross your arms: At chest level, criss-cross arms back and forth. Do 15 times.

Now, go and tackle the day with vim and vigor.

We like rituals - for us, that's the only way you stay committed to our program.

Jaime's FIT 3:

Every morning Jaime starts his day with these 3 fitness moves:

1. Do regular push-ups, or on your knees, or even on the wall, if needed. Start with 20 each day. Do them every day and that's 600 push-ups for the month.

Push Ups on Knees

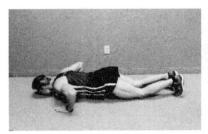 

Push Ups on Wall

2. Do 20 squats to work your legs and get your heart pumping. 20 squats a day gives you 600 squats to tone your legs for the month.

Squats

You can also use a chair for balance. Hit your behind on the seat on each repetition-like you're sitting up.

3. Do horizontal Planks, modified on your knees, or up on your arms for 1 minute. You can also by place your elbows on a table, leaning forward and holding. That gives you 30 minutes of AB work for the month to help you get a slimmer, trimmer, tighter waistline.

Horizontal Planks

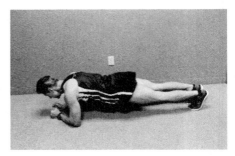

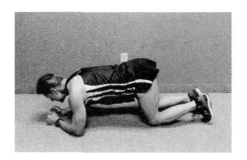

Modified on your Knees

Up on your Arms

7 Days Without Fitness Makes One Weak

Think about that saying. Make time for your program. We've found over the years if you start your week off by working out on Mondays, you kick start your healthy week ahead.

Increase your Muscle Mass

Some women are concerned that by increasing bone mass, they will get muscles like a man, or like Arnold Schwarzenegger (or Jack). On the contrary, lifting weights will lower your chances for osteoporosis, and will get you lean, strong, trim and healthy. Strive for a toned body.

Many people who suffer from the loss of a high amount of muscle mass on a calorie-restricted diet actually look WORSE because without exercise, the muscles become weak and flabby. How disappointing is that? So, the

Keep in mind, squeezing in only eight minutes of physical exercise per day will result in huge benefits to your health, give you more energy, and perk up your mood. More strength makes daily life easier, gives you better balance and fewer falls, strengthens the heart, and makes you look and feel younger.

You also won't be as likely to gain excess body fat should you overeat, because you are going to be burning it off more quickly than someone with less muscle mass. As mentioned earlier, a pound of muscle takes up less space than a pound of fat. Lean body mass uses five times the calories as fat mass. That's why we see people who lose two dress sizes or two pants sizes with a five-pound weight loss. And it's why we think it is so important you are aware that increasing your metabolism is the most effective way to burn fat.

tendency is to go back to old habits. Imagine you go on a diet – restrict your food intake, watch the scale numbers drop down, then end up hating the way you look. Not a good scenario!

You may look slimmer and better in clothes after your restricted diet, but check your mirror with all your clothes off – you will be able to see significant amounts of excess fat around various points of your body. Losing weight is quite different from losing fat and that's one of the problems with muscle mass loss, which only sets you up for a future of inactivity.

Borrowed Wisdom: On Receiving Criticism

When criticized, I've learned to look into myself and if I find a seed of truth, I try to be cognizant and improve on the criticism. There are certain habits that we accumulate as we grow older, and some are annoying to others. Have you ever asked a friend to be honest with you, and all of the sudden you're unhappy with the answer, and you become indignant and on the defensive? If you don't let your ego get in the way or get down on yourself, you can let it go and move on. Imperfections are part of being human.

~Elaine

Chapter 7: BOOMERS. The Daily 8

T he program that we designed for you can be completed in ONLY 8 minutes. Most exercises are performed for 40 seconds, which is approximately 15 repetitions (reps). A rep is the number of times you perform a specific exercise. Some of the exercises that are performed on one side of the body will be noted by 10 repetitions or times each side. You'll see photographs of each of these exercises, so you can see what proper form looks like.

*Beginners, move at your own pace – especially when you're just starting out. It's perfectly okay not to finish all 40 seconds or 15 reps at once. You want to start slowly, and build up your strength and stamina.

This routine is carried out by performing a set of one exercise first, then moving directly to a different exercise, and then another, and then another, all with little or no rest between sets. The idea is to keep your heart rate elevated (see table on page 54 for heart rate target zones) so that you'll continue burning a maximum number of calories as you tone your muscles with resistance training and body conditioning.

The Daily 8 allows you to get an optimum program in the least amount of time. How? By "fusing" constant movement exercises with resistance training. You will be utilizing multiple muscle groups – in essence, working out two fitness components at the same time, without resting between each exercise transition.

Why will this work?

The non-impact routine reduces the stress on your joints. It also greatly improves your power and endurance simultaneously, making you stronger and more physically fit — all the while putting on lean muscle and sculpting a lean, healthy physique. It's a win/win proposition.

We will let you know in parenthesis which body part each movement works. There are 12 movements performed each day for approximately 40 seconds which gives you a total body workout in 8 minutes.

Fitness Fusion

Borrowed Wisdom: On Exercise

I was thinking the other day of what I have observed with my friends that had a positive attitude and a real zest for life, those who exercised and those who didn't. My friends that remained active lived a long life and some are still alive. The ones that didn't exercise and didn't care about what they put in their mouths died early, or they lived long, but they always had an ailment and became very weak and ended up in nursing homes. Several lost their memories. That's one thing I have observed.

~Elaine

"First we inspire them, then we perspire them."

Jack LaLanne

Ageless Energy and Timeless Health Exercises

Day 1 Fast Fitness

1. **Cardio**-marchingorjoggingin place, jumping jacks, jumping rope, or throwing punches. Do 40 seconds. (heart)

2. **Push Ups on Wall -** is literally a vertical push up. Stand in front of a wall about two feet away from it with your legs spread to shoulder width apart. Lean forward with your arms extended to shoulder width and try to touch your nose to the wall or door. Do 15 reps or times. (chest, shoulders, back of the arm)

3.   **Butt Kicks** - Place your hands on a chair, keep one leg straight and lift opposite leg smoothly upward. Not too high. Do 10 reps each side. (buns)

4.   **Seated Ab Twisters**: Sitting toward the edge of a chair. Place hands behind head. Lift right knee toward left elbow -then lift left knee toward right elbow. Alternating to the count of 30 reps. (abs and love handles)

5. **Lateral Raise** - Start with the resistance at your side. Slowly raise the resistance out to your sides until they reach shoulder level. Your palms should be faced down, like your pouring tea. Your elbows should be slightly bent throughout this slow and controlled movement. Do 15 reps. (outside middle shoulders)

6. **Side Lunges-** Stand erect, hands on hips (or chair for balance) lunge to the side. Make sure knees line up with toes. Step back repeat for 10 reps each leg. (hips, thighs and buns)

Cardio - marching or jogging in place
ing rope, or throwing punches. Do 40
seconds. (heart)

7. **Bent Over Rows-** bending over at the waist, knees
    slightly bent, extend both arms downward then slowly
    pull them up towards your chest-smoothly. Do 15 reps.
    (upper back)

8. **Tricep Kicks-** Bend forward at your waist and bring the weight up by keeping your elbow next to your torso. Slowly straighten the arm out and make sure that you don't lock out the elbow joint. The KEY is to keep your elbow up for a full range of motion. Slow and steady movements. Do 15 reps. (back of the arms)

9. **Jack's One Arm Dead Lifts-**One of Jack's favorites. Stand with your feet hip-width apart. With left hand behind your back, keeping right arm straight, slowly pick up a weight, which is in front of right toe. Slowly lift weight smoothly up in front of right leg and as you come to the standing position. Keep your back straight and abs tight. No Jerking! Do 10 reps each side. (buns, back of your legs and lower back)

10. **Shoulder Press -** Slightly bend knees, while keeping your abs tight and back straight. Hold weights just above your shoulder level. Keep your palms faced out. Press the resistance straight up until they're almost touching. Don't lock out your elbows. Do 15 reps. (shoulders)

11. **Cardio** - marching or jogging in place, jumping jacks, jumping rope, or throwing punches. Do 40 seconds. (heart)

Day 2 Strength Aerobics

1.   **Cardio** - marching or jogging in place, jumping jacks, jumping rope, or throwing punches. Do 40 seconds. (heart)

2.   **Standing Rows** – Slightly bend knees and keep your back straight. Slowly lift weight to chest height and then pull the weights back like you're rowing a boat. Pull your shoulders back and keep your chest out. Try not to lean back. This is a steady, controlled movement. Do 15 reps. (firms up the "bra strap" line and the back)

3. **Plie Squats** -Standing up, place your feet in the 10 o'clock and 2 o'clock position. Slowly lower your body into a squat position like you're sitting in a seat and repeat. Keep your knees in line with your toes. Do 15 reps. (buns, inner thighs, and back of legs)

4. **Bicep Curls** - Stand with your knees slightly bent, abs tight, and keep your back straight. Feet hip-width apart. Hold the hand-held weights on the outside of your thighs. Slowly curl the weights up toward your shoulders. Controlled movement --don't swing your arms. Do 15 reps. (front of your arms)

5. **Windmills -** Arms stretched out. Bend forward at the waist touching your right hand to your left foot and alternating by touching left hand to your right foot. Do 10 reps each side. (waist, lower back)

6. **Cardio** - marching or jogging in place, jumping jacks, jumping rope, or throwing punches. Do 40 seconds. (heart)

7. **Alternating Lunges** Standing with your feet slightly apart – slowly step with right foot forward into a lunge movement. Don't allow your front knee to go past the toes and keep the knee aligned with your toes. Keep your abs tight –and back straight. Alternate legs by lunging forward with your left foot – continue alternating legs. Think of this movement like a "fencer" in the Olympics. Do 10 reps each leg. (hips, buns, quads and back of legs)

8. **Shoulder Press** - Slightly bend knees, while keeping your abs tight and back straight. Hold weights just above your shoulder level. Keep your palms faced out. Press the resistance straight up until they're almost touching. Don't lock out your elbows. Do 15 reps. (shoulders)

9.   **Standing Twisters** – Standing. Bring your right elbow to your lifted left knee and then reverse by bringing your left elbow to your lifted right knee. Keep repeating for 30 reps. (core)

10. **Tricep Presses:** Begin with arms at your side, holding a weight in each hand, bring back both arms as far as possible, hold and release. Don't swing. Do 15 reps. (back of the arm)

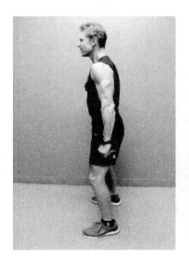

11. **Reverse Lunges -** We recommend using a chair for balance and support.

    Stand with your feet slightly apart. Slowly step back about 2-3 feet. Bend both of your knees – and lower yourself in a controlled movement. Don't allow your front knee to bend over your toe. Do 10 reps each side. (hips, buns, thighs)

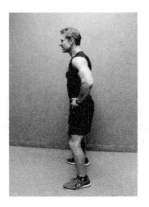 

12. **Cardio** - marching or jogging in place, jumping jacks, jumping rope, or throwing punches. Do 40 seconds. (heart)

Day 3 Floor Fitness

On Knees –if you can't get on your knees –please stand and do these movements

1. **Modified Push Ups.** On your hands and knees, slowly lower yourself -about three or four inches from the floor. Your elbows should be bent at 90 degrees. Keep your abs tight and your back straight throughout the movement, and gently push yourself up without locking the elbows. Do 15 reps. (chest, shoulders and back of the arms)

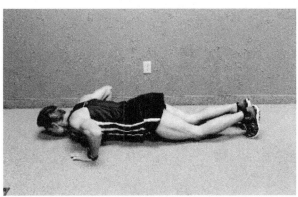

2. **Buns Lifts** -On your elbows and knees on the floor. Extend one leg straight and just lift that leg until it's parallel with the floor. Don't lift up too high-and don't arch your back. Slowly lower and control the movements so you're not swinging the leg. Do 10 reps each leg. (buns)

3. **Bicep Curls on knees-** Hold the hand-held weights on the outside of your thighs. Slowly curl the weights up toward your shoulders. Controlled movement --don't swing your arms. Do 15 reps. (front of your arms)

4. **Planks** -Do horizontal, modified on your knees, or Up on your Arms planks. Extend body on floor, up on toes and elbows and hold position for 40 seconds. (Abs).

Horizontal Planks

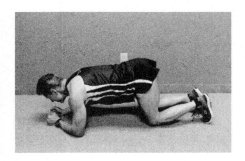

Modified on your Knees

Up on your Arms

5. **Tricep Presses on Knees:** Begin with arms at your side, holding a weight in each hand, bring back both arms as far as possible, hold and release. Don't swing. Do 15 reps. (back of the arm)

6. **Superman Pose**-Lying on stomach, lift opposite arm and opposite leg at the same time and hold for a count. Alternate arms and legs 10 reps each side. (lower back muscles)

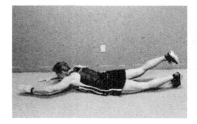 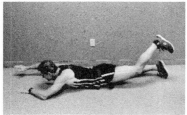

Lying On Your Back

7. **Bridges Pelvic Tilt-** Lie on our back, knees bent, arms and hands straight at your sides. Now lift your hips up off the floor so that you form a straight line from your knees to your shoulders. Lower yourself and repeat 15 reps. (buns, back of your legs)

 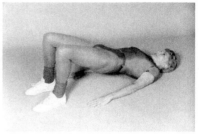

8. **Crunches -**On your back with your knees bent at 90 degrees. Place your hands just behind your ears–this will ensure that you don't pull on your neck. Slowly lift your shoulders off the floor-you don't have to go up too high. Do 15 reps slow and controlled. (abs)

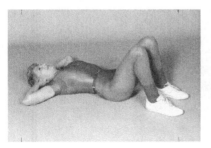 

9. **Quad Lifts** -On the floor on your back. Keep one knee bent at 90 degrees and straighten your opposite leg and lift it up until perpendicular to floor (or as high as you can). Slowly lower your leg back to the starting position. Tighten your abs to keep your back from arching. Do 10 reps each side. (front of thighs and hip flexors)

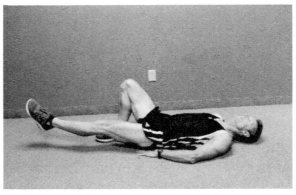

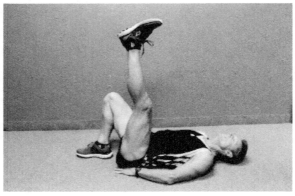

10. **Pullovers-**Lie on bed, bench or floor. Extend the weight (held in both hands) above your head keeping your arms straight. Lower the weight down behind your head, pause and slowly raise the weight until it is once again perpendicular to the floor. Make sure you do these smoothly, do not jerk. Do 15 reps. (back)

11. **Scissors-** Lie on back on floor. Spread legs wide and cross one leg over the other in a repetitive motion. Keep your abs tight. Do 30 reps. (inner thigh)

12. **Bicycles** –Lying on your back–your knees are up and bent at 90 degrees. Place your fingers behind your ears-don't pull on your neck. Slowly bring your knees into your chest –alternating each leg to opposite elbow –in a pedaling motion. Your right elbow goes to your left knee and left elbow to the right knee. Do 30 reps. (Abs)

Day 4 Chair Fitness

1. **Cardio** - marching or jogging in place, jumping jacks, jumping rope, or throwing punches. Do 40 seconds. (heart)

2. **Pushups on Chair-** With your legs planted shoulder width apart, bend at the waist, and grasp the sides of the chair(that is not likely to move as you put pressure on it.) Lower your head and try to touch your nose to the seat of the chair. Push back up and repeat 15 reps. (chest, back of the arms, shoulders)

3. **Butt Kicks -** Place your hands on a chair, keep one leg straight and lift leg smoothly upward. Not too high. Do 10 reps each side. (buns)

4. **Woodchops-** Bend knees slightly and clasp hands together with or without a weight. Swing hands up to the side as far as possible feeling the twist in your torso. Repeat from side to side. Do 10 reps each side. (core)

5. **Dead Lifts (two arms)-** Stand with your feet hip-width apart. Slowly tip over from your hips and lower your body as far as your flexibility allows. Slowly raise up. Keep your back straight and abs tight. Don't round your back. No Jerking ! Do 15 reps. (buns, back of your legs and lower back

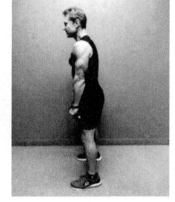

6. **Dips on Chair -** Sitting on a chair, placing your hands next to your hips. Lift your hips off the chair and slowly lower your body until your elbows are at 90 degrees and then lift yourself back up. Keep your knees bent throughout the movement. However, if you're advanced – you can straighten your legs. Keep your body close to the chair when you're lowering it. Do 15 reps. (back of arms)

7. **Cardio -** marching or jogging in place, jump ing jacks, jumping rope, or throwing punches. Do 40 seconds. (heart)

8. **Outer Thigh Lifts** You'll need a chair for balance and support. Standing up straight slowly lift your leg straight out and lower. Keep your abs tight and your back straight. Try not to lean during the movement. Slow and controlled movements. Do 10 reps each side. (outer hip)

9. **Bent Over Rows-** bending over at the waist, knees slightly bent, extend both arms downward then slowly pull them up towards your chest-smoothly. Do 15 reps. (upper back)

10. **Squats-** Your feet should be shoulder width apart. Your abs are held in tight and your back is straight. Place your hands out in front about chest level. Slowly lower yourself into a seating position. Make sure your knees don't go past your toes and are aligned straight. Do 15 reps. (buns, thighs, hamstrings and quads)

11. **Ab Raises on Chair-** Sit on edge of armless chair. Extend legs out in front of you. Now bring knees together to your chest, pause and lower legs back to floor. Do 15 reps. (abs)

12. **Cardio -** marching or jogging in place, jumping jacks, jumping rope, or throwing punches. Do 40 seconds. (heart)

Day 5 Fitness Fusion

1. **Cardio -** marching or jogging in place, jumping jacks, jumping rope, or throwing punches. Do 40 seconds. (heart)

2. **Chest Flys Standing:** With or without weights. Place fists in front of chest with elbows high, extend both arms out as far as possible and then bring arms in and out like you're hugging a tree. Do 15 reps. (outer chest, shoulders)

3. **Side Lunges-** Stand erect, hands on hips (or chair for balance) lunge to the side. Make sure knees line up with toes. Step back repeat for 10 reps each leg. (hips, thighs and buns)

4. **Lateral Raise-** Start with the resistance at your side. Slowly raise the resistance out to your sides until they reach shoulder level. Your palms should be faced down, like your pouring tea. Your elbows should be slightly bent throughout this slow and controlled movement. Do 15 reps. (outside middle shoulders)

5. **Jack's One Arm Dead Lifts-**One of Jack's favorites. Stand with your feet hip-width apart. With left hand behind your back, keeping right arm straight, slowly pick up a weight, which is in front of right toe. Slowly lift weight smoothly up in front of right leg and as you come to the standing position. Keep your back straight and abs tight. No Jerking ! Do 10 reps each side. (buns, back of your legs and lower back)

6. **Cardio -** marching or jogging in place, jumping jacks, jumping rope, or throwing punches. Do 40 seconds. (heart)

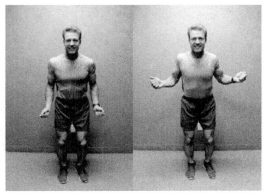

7. **Triceps Overhead Extension** Standing straight with your knees slightly bent and your abs held tight. Clasp both hands behind head, and extend your arms overhead. Keep your elbows close to your ears and slowly lower weights behind you – until your elbows are at 90 degrees. Do 15 reps. (back of the arm)

8. **Plie Squats** -Standing up, place your feet in the 10 o'clock and 2 o'clock position. Slowly lower your body into a squat position like you're sitting in a seat and repeat. Keep your knees in line with your toes. Do 15 reps. (buns, inner thighs, and back of legs)

9. **Bicep Curls -** Stand with your knees slightly bent, abs tight, and keep your back straight. Feet hip-width apart. Hold the hand-held weights on the outside of your thighs. Slowly curl the weights up toward your shoulders. Controlled movement --don't swing your arms. Do 15 reps. (front of your arms)

10. **Alternating Lunges** Standing with your feet together – slowly step with right foot forward into a lunge movement. Don't allow your front knee to go past the toes and keep the knee aligned with your toes. Keep your abs tight –and back straight. Alternate legs by lunging forward with your left foot – continue alternating legs. Think of this movement like a "fencer" in the Olympics. Do 10 reps each side. (hips, buns, quads and back of legs.

11. **Shoulder Press -** Slightly bend knees, while keeping your abs tight and back straight. Hold weights just above your shoulder level. Keep your palms faced out. Press the resistance straight up until they're almost touching. Don't lock out your elbows. Do 15 reps. (shoulders)

12. **Cardio -** marching or jogging in place, jumping jacks, jumping rope, or throwing punches. Do 40 seconds. (heart)

PART THREE: REFUEL

"Exercise is King, Nutrition is Queen. Put them together and you have a Kingdom."

Jack LaLanne

Chapter 8: BOOMERS. Eat in Moderation

*Y*our Fork and Spoon will be your BEST pieces of Fitness Equipment.* We can do plenty of damage with those two weapons of mass expansion, the fork and spoon. So, proper portions and proportions of your favorite foods will be paramount. Notice we didn't say diet?

Our society has become overfed. We overeat on a daily basis because our food landscape has changed. The world of fast food, restaurant food, prepared food, and mammoth portions of food make it difficult to keep a calorie count within a healthy range. Studies have shown, over the past few decades, portion sizes of everything from pizza to bagels to soft drinks have inflated by an average of two to five times in America. Result? An expanding waistline!

"What you eat in private, you eventually wear in public."

Moderation is Key

Supersizing has become the norm at restaurants, not only at fast food houses. We all want a "bang for our buck" so it's an easy marketing tool for restaurants to fill you up on starches (like bread, rice and pasta) while keeping the perception that you're getting heaping plates of food for your money.

If a restaurant served you a proper single serving of pasta - the size of your fist - you might never come back. We wrongly equate value to portion size, and this attitude towards food gets us into BIG trouble.

Our lifestyles are partially to blame. Think about your own life right now: Do you eat on the run, eat at your desk, or eat in front of the TV? Most of us take part in some, if not all, of these behaviors. Some eat out an average of four nights per week. Unless you have the budget to frequent nouvelle-cuisine restaurants where portions are controlled, you're being overfed impossible-to-eat, abnormal portions. This may sound unrealistic to you right now, but an appetizer is a true sensible portion size for your stomach.

We're convinced the reason for this portion problem is that we don't know what a single serving size of anything should look like. And yet, controlling portion sizes may be the single most effective thing you can do to promote lasting leanness!

Once you get a sense of proper serving sizes, you'll be delighted with the changes you see in your body and the satisfaction you feel in your health. You'll find that you can now control your weight, and balance your food budget, without starving yourself of nutrition by going on a fad diet.

Borrowed Wisdom: On Relaxation vs. Tension

Looking back on my life, I've always been one to take on a lot of responsibility. Consequently, it caused a lot of tension, plus dealing with set-backs and people who shirked their duty, a lot rested on my shoulders. The jobs got done but with a lot of stress. I didn't complain, but I noticed I really didn't know how to really relax. Jack could relax anywhere, anytime. Even when he would film 10 shows in a day after doing his live show in the morning, between shows he would find a table and lie quietly on it until the next show. His answer to relaxing was his workouts. I started to do more workouts and I receive regular massages which made all the difference in my life. I continue it to this day.

~Elaine

Portion Power

Instead of weighing or measuring cups and spoons try the "Jaime Brenkus eyeball" method for instantly measuring portions by just using your eyes and hands.

Jaime devised a patented portion-control plate, with the help of a Registered Dietitian from the Cleveland Clinic. In a few short weeks, you should become a portion expert who's able to "eyeball" meals. We've found that it's so easy to portion your foods, instead of measuring so there is no need to weigh your foods or use measuring cups and spoons. Many of us don't have time for that. This is so simple and can be applied to any food choices that you make. The following visuals were based on the plate.

The "Jaime Brenkus eyeball" method

There is no need to overcomplicate portions. Start by using your eyes and your hands.

You have the best measuring unit within your grasp. Yes, your hand is your easy portion control plan.

To devise a lean meal every time:

- Your palm determines your protein portions / 3 or 4 ounces

- Your fist determines your vegetable portions

- Your cupped hand determines your carb portions

- Your thumb determines your fat portions

To devise a lean meal every time:

Borrowed Wisdom: On Motivation

Since we are focusing some attention on inspiration and motivation, I wanted to share this with you. While I was in college, I wanted to do some photos for ads as a model. I was told that I was too short for that type of modeling. So, I positioned myself as a fitness/athletic candidate, where height didn't matter. I went on and did over 100 ad photos, posters, book covers, and magazine covers while I was in Tampa, honing in on an attainable look – not bodybuilding, but toned for these types of photos.

It set the stage for me to believe at a very core level that one should never, ever give up and always believe that you can do anything even when the naysayers think you can't. There are always more ways to bringing your objectives to fruition.

When you come to a bump in the road and you know you can't go over it... just go around it and never compromise your dreams and vision.

~Jaime

Therefore, if you're still eating most of the same foods you were before, you should be able to make fairly accurate estimates. For example, once you've portioned a 3-ounce pork chop 15 times, you know what it looks like. You don't need to measure it – just 'eyeball' it. It will become second nature.

80/20 Rule. Follow our 80/20 rule, which is not exactly 100% perfection with everything you eat, but it gives you room for some errors. No one's perfect. And it's like what

Jack said: "It's not what you do some of the time, it's what you do most of the time." So, do your best, stay on target, and you can get away with a little indulgence.

Here's a little hint. Ask yourself when you're about to put food in your mouth, "What is this food going to do for me? Will this food choice get me closer to my goal or move me further away? If you say closer_80% of the time, you are eating healthy choices. If you are eating not-so-healthy foods 20% of the time, you can still be lean.

Jack was fond of saying, "The food you eat today is walking and talking tomorrow." We literally become what we eat. The lean style is built on a bedrock of common sense, and proven effective by real-world results.

Perfection is not always possible, but what's great about the concept of being 80% "loyal to lean" is that it allows for slip-ups. Remember, a slip is not a fall. No one's perfect. If you're eating meals that aren't as healthy as you intended, no worries – just "dust yourself off, pick yourself up" and choose a healthier choice the next meal.

Calorie Exchange. We recommend you limit special occasion foods, such as candy bars, cookies and other sweets. Practice moderation when consuming beer and wine, limit yourself to three times per week, and pre-plan as often as possible. These foods and beverages provide lots of extra calories with very few vitamins and minerals. Sharp label reading skills are a must with your favorite snacks! First, read the calories per serving. You can always adjust the serving size to keep the calories where you want them. The following list gives examples of 100-200 calorie items that can be worked into a day instead of adding on any additional calories for the day.

You can safely allow for one of the following special occasion foods if you <u>omit a serving of your usual starch at one meal</u>. For example, if you want some ice cream after dinner, try not to eat a serving of pasta during that meal.

Snacks

Here are a few tasty snack choices (not that we recommend them) when that sweet tooth hits or when you're in between meals. Just remember, this is just your calorie education from one of our trusted dietitians. Use **the below** list **only** with the above **20%** exchange system.

Snacks between 100-200 calories:

- 1/2 cup of ice cream or sherbet

- 1/8 single crusted fruit or custard pie

- 2 small sized candy bars

- 2- 2 1/2" diameter cookies

- 1-3/4 x 3/4 cube of cheese

- 3 cups non-air popped popcorn

- 12 ounce soft drink

- 12 ounce juice drink

- 1/4 cup mixed nuts

- 1 granola bar

- 8-12 crackers

- 1 handful of nuts

- 4 oz. low-fat cottage cheese

- 1 oz. of raisins

- 8 oz. of skim milk latte

- 8 small rectangles of Graham crackers

- 48 thin pretzel sticks

When Elaine had just met Jack, before they even dated, she walked in the TV studio with her favorite chocolate donut and Jack's remark was, "The only thing good thing about the donut is the hole in the middle!" This thought resonated with Elaine, and she hasn't had a donut since!

More can be Less. When it comes to weight and inch loss, most people preoccupy themselves with the notion of 'less food.' It's always, "You can't have this – you can't have that – eat less." Don't focus on eating **LESS**. Focus on the word **MORE** good food and **MORE** Probiotics.

Putting the "New" in Nutrition

Probiotics and Your Microbiome

Research on Probiotics and your microbiome has exploded in the past few decades.

Probiotics are foods that contain live bacteria that replace or add to the beneficial bacteria normally in the digestive tract. In a nut shell, Probiotics are often called the "good" or "helpful" bacteria because they keep your gut healthy. Examples are yogurt, kefir, fresh sauerkraut, miso, sourdough bread, and many cheeses. Also, whole grains, beans, and more plant protein. You have probably noticed that more and more products have Probiotics on their labels.

In your gut you have a separate group of cells (other than the trillions of cells that inhabit your body) called microbiome. This separate community of cells in our guts have trillions more cells of microbes and can have a beneficial or negative effect on your health. These trillions of cells are continually replacing themselves or populating with other microbes. If your diet is unhealthy, as these cells populate with other microbes you will find yourself with an unhealthy gut prone to disease. Therefore, if your diet is healthy and also contains probiotic foods, you will benefit by having a healthy immune system and overall metabolism.

Studies indicate that sedentary people have different microbes than active people. Past research indicates that an unhealthy gut can have a significant impact on the way you think, feel, and act. In fact, more studies have shown that a sedentary, unhealthy gut has been instrumental in the occurrence of obesity, depression and bone density. However, those same studies reveal that people who exercised and followed a healthy diet prevented inflammation and bolstered their immune system. So, you have two paths to choose from, a sedentary one that is wearing out, or one that is continually being renewed.

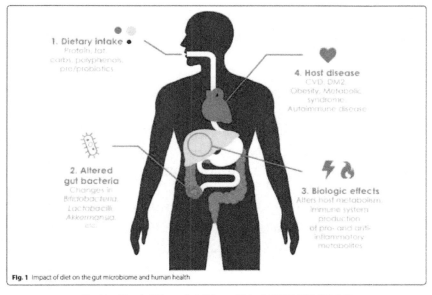

1. Dietary intake
Protein, fat,
carbs, polyphenols,
pre/probiotics

4. Host disease
CVD, DM2,
Obesity, Metabolic
syndrome,
Autoimmune disease

2. Altered gut bacteria
Changes in
Bifidobacteria,
Lactobacilli,
Akkermansia,
etc.

3. Biologic effects
Alters host metabolism,
immune system
production
of pro- and anti-
inflammatory
metabolites

Fig. 1 Impact of diet on the gut microbiome and human health

Credit: Singh RK et al. / J Transl Med 2017 (CC BY 4.0)

Remodel your thoughts. Your body is like a piece of clay — you can mold it and shape as you desire. By concentrating on eating more of these choices — all of which are *very* filling — most people naturally start eating less unhealthy foods. We eat fewer calories by crowding them out with more nutritious foods that are also high in fiber and increase your satiety – or the feeling of fullness. And by focusing on eating **MORE** instead of less, we're less likely to be hungry and less likely to feel like we're denying ourselves things.

Concentrate on remodeling your thinking to eating **MORE** of these food groups and doing **MORE** of these activities:

- **MORE** Vegetables: Eat an abundant variety, the more, the better.

- **MORE** Fruits: Choose a rainbow of fruits every day.

- **MORE** Whole Grains: Choose whole grains, such as old-fashioned rolled oats, or steel-cut oats, whole-grain bread, and brown rice.

- **MORE** Healthy Proteins: Choose fish, poultry, lean meats, beans, or nuts, which contain healthful nutrients, generally less fat and more fiber.

- **MORE** Healthy Oils: Use extra-virgin olive, and other plant oils in cooking, on salads, and at the table, since these healthy fats reduce harmful cholesterol and are good for the heart.

- **MORE** Water: Drink water or tea. These are your best fluids to keep you rehydrated.

- **MORE** Movement. Get up and move. It doesn't have to be formal fitness. Anytime you move, you burn calories.

- **MORE** Sleep. Studies show that when you get in 7-8 hours per night it reduces the risk for obesity.

- **MORE** Salads. Get used to ordering a salad at every meal—it's all about helping fill the stomach, and that means eat your salad first before the main course; you will feel full longer.

Do calories actually count? If you take in fewer calories than your body needs, you lose. So, there must be some control of your calories to balance your energy and weight.

First, know how many calories you should be consuming on a daily basis. Your Doctor or Health Professional can help you with this, but as an example, women over age 50 who are moderately active need about 1,500 to 1,700 calories per day. Your needs can vary based on several factors, like physical activity, current muscle mass, and even genetics. Cutting back calories will help you lose weight, but you want to avoid cutting out too many to avoid getting fatigued and even slowing down your metabolism further.

Changing the types of foods you eat is also important, too. Choosing healthy foods like fruits and vegetables over sugary or salty snacks, whole grains over white flour, getting adequate calcium and incorporating lean proteins will give you more energy and help you stay healthy. Also, make sure to drink plenty of water throughout the day to stay hydrated.

Calories count, but you don't always have to count them. However, it is helpful to have an idea of what the calorie count on certain foods are, such as a potato at 150 calories. But, stuffed potato skins are about 400 calories. One slice of Cheddar Cheese is about 110 calories, but a slice of 2% Sharp Cheddar is only 50 calories. No matter what, it still comes down to either storing calories or expending calories.

The Downsize

Research reaffirms that minimizing your plate, bowl, or drinking glass drastically cuts down on your portion sizes. It is common sense, if you eat from a larger bowl, you'll most likely eat more food. Think about your own table habits, we believe we're all guilty of this "Super Bowl" mentality.

Cut Calories, Shed Pounds

Numbers don't lie, even if you cut a mere 100 calories every day, your body will respond positively. The calories you don't consume are the same calories you don't have to expend. If your goal is to lose weight or inches, your body will need to have a negative caloric balance, so you either have to take in less calories OR burn those calories through activity. Period.

"Getting lean isn't about CHANCE... It's about CHOICE."

Jaime Brenkus

How to Cut 100 Calories

- Use salsa or a dollop of Greek yogurt on a baked potato instead of sour cream

- Don't have a piece of bread/roll with butter

- Remove the skin from chicken before or after cooking

- Use smaller amounts of light mayo or plain yogurt instead of full-fat mayo for sandwiches or tuna salad

- Drink water with lemon wedges instead of soft drinks

- Leave 3-4 bites of food on your plate at each meal and don't have second servings

- Fill up on a piece of fruit instead of drinking 8 ounces of your favorite juice

- Put a handful of your favorite snack into a bowl, roll up the bag, and then put the bag back into the pantry

- Use a non-stick skillet or cooking spray instead of butter when stove-top cooking

- Choose tuna packed in water instead of tuna packed in oil

- Don't add croutons to your salads

- Reduce your portion of pasta and/or rice by ½ cup

- Choose thin-crust pizza as opposed to thick-crust

- Top your pizza with vegetables, not fatty meats like sausage and pepperoni, and do not order double cheese

- Choose 1 cup of oatmeal instead of 1 ½ cups of cereal with 2% milk

- Grill a vegetable burger or turkey burger instead of a beef burger

- Replace your breaded fish sticks with grilled fresh fish

- Replace your daily candy bar with a piece of fresh fruit

Lean Ways to Slash and Smash Calories

Lean happens when you start with one meal at a time and make minor, smart substitutions or changes in portion sizes. Below are suggestions and how to accomplish this goal.

Lean Breakfast

- Ditch the glazed donut and eat a bagel instead. *Save 93 calories!*

- Eat 3/4 cup oatmeal instead of 1-1/2 cups of oatmeal. *Save 97 calories!*

- Substitute 3 oz. of turkey sausage for a serving of pork sausage. *Save 120 calories!*

- Grab a small bagel instead of a medium bagel. *Save 99 calories!*

- Spread your whole grain waffles with 2 tablespoons of maple syrup instead of 1 tablespoon of margarine or butter. *Save 110 calories!*

- Top your whole grain bagel with 1.5 oz. of fat-free cream cheese in lieu of regular. *Save 108 calories!*

- Try 1 oz. of maple turkey bacon instead of maple pork bacon. *Save 118 calories!*

Lean Lunch & Dinner

- Instead of 3 oz. of crispy fried chicken with skin, eat 3 oz. baked chicken with skin. *Save approximately 102 calories!*

- Choose a slice of thin crust pizza over thick crust pizza. *Save 106 calories!*

- Forget broccoli cheddar soup. A 7-oz portion of vegetable soup is better. *Save 119 calories!*

- Cut a 6 oz. steak in half and take the other portion home for another meal. *Save 111 calories!*

- Order a skinless chicken breast instead of chicken with skin. *Save 102 calories!*

- Build a sandwich with1.5 oz. of deli turkey breast instead of 1.5 oz. hard salami. *Save 119 calories!*

- Enjoy 12 oz. of steamed rice (choose brown rice when possible) as an alternative to fried rice. *Save 96 calories!*

- Eat only half of your hamburger or sandwich bun. *Save 100 calories! Or, put your burger on a lettuce wrap.*

Lean Snacks and Sides

- Eat 2 oz. pretzels instead of the same size portion of potato chips. *Save 94 calories!*

- Bake 2 oz. of oven fries in lieu of 2 oz. of fast food fries. *Save 88 calories!*

- Forgo a 6-oz portion of potato chips and eat 6 oz. of tortilla chips instead. ***Save 96 calories!***

- Dip 1 cup celery into your favorite salsa or hummus instead of 1 oz. of tortilla chips. ***Save 125 calories!***

- Eat an entire medium apple instead of a small (5 oz.) candy apple. ***Save 118 calories!***

- Snack on 1 oz. of baked potato chips instead of regular chips. ***Save 90 calories!***

- Choose 3 oz. of mozzarella cheese for your sandwich instead of Swiss cheese. ***Save 108 calories!***

- Swap 1 cup of canned pineapple in heavy syrup for crushed pineapple in water. ***Save 119 calories!***

- Say no to 1 oz. of deep-fried onion rings and instead enjoy 1 oz. of grilled onions with your meal. ***Save 92 calories!***

- Try 1.5 oz. of fresh grapes instead of 1.5 oz. of raisins. ***Save 98 calories!***

- Enjoy a healthy 8-oz. baked potato instead of 8 oz. of French fries. ***Save 104 calories!***

Lean Sweets & Desserts

- Serve low-fat ice cream in a dish instead of a waffle cone. ***Save 121 calories!***

- Try a healthier nutrition bar instead of a peanut candy bar. *Save 94 calories!*

- Leave that 1/2 cup of strawberry ice cream in the freezer. Enjoy 1/2 cup of fresh strawberries topped with 2 Tbsp. of fat-free whipped cream as an alternative. *Save 102 calories!*

- Substitute 5 oz. of apple pie, with 5 oz. of baked apple crisp. *Save 85 calories!*

- Instead of 4 oz. of regular chocolate pudding, enjoy a sugar-free portion. *Save 92 calories!*

Lean Beverages

- Instead of 1 cup of prepared lemonade, try 1 cup of a sugar-free variety. *Save 103 calories!*

- Prepare your coffee with 4 oz. of fat-free half and half instead of regular half and half. *Save 88 calories!*

- Enjoy 5 oz. of chocolate milk instead of 5 oz. of a chocolate milkshake *Save 110 calories!*

- Split a 20 oz. bottle of regular soda and save for later *Save 120 calories!*

- Drink 1 cup of diet soda instead of 1 cup of regular soda. *Save 97 calories!*

- Swap a 12-oz. glass of skim milk for whole milk. *Save 96 calories!*

- Drink two 12-oz. light beers instead of two regular beers. *Save 100 calories!*

Lean Condiments and Sauces

- Top your salad with 1.5 oz. reduced-fat Italian dressing instead of regular. *Save 96 calories!*

- Try either 1 oz. of cheese (140 cal.) *or* 10 croutons (60 cal.) on your salad—not both. *Save 60-140 calories!*

- Instead of 3 oz. of regular sour cream, use a fat-free variety **or plain nonfat yogurt**. *Save 120 calories!*

- Use 2 Tbsp. reduced-fat light mayonnaise instead of regular mayonnaise. *Save 102 calories!*

- Dip your salad in a side of ranch dressing (2 tsp.) instead of pouring 2 Tbsp. of dressing on the salad. *Save 97 calories!*

- Skip the 5 oz. of Alfredo sauce and eat a whopping 7 oz. of marinara sauce. *Save 129 calories!*

- Add flavor to vegetables with 3 oz. of hot sauce — not 1 oz. of bleu cheese dressing. *Save 117 calories!*

Once you get a sense of serving sizes, you'll be delighted with the results and satisfaction. You'll find that you can now control your weight and balance your nutritional budget without starving yourself or going on fad diets.

"He that stuffeth… puffeth!"

Jack LaLanne

Clean Plate Club

Don't stuff yourself! Eat to the point of being satisfied – not stuffed, and then…**STOP!**

Jack LaLanne on the American Diet. "Would you get your dog up every day, give him a cup of coffee, a donut, and a cigarette? Hell, no. You'd kill the damn dog."

There's an Old Chinese saying, "Eat until you're eight-tenths full." You don't have to finish everything on your plate simply because it's there. Eat until you're about 80% full.

Think comfortable - not full. The small, simple changes you make have the most dramatic and lasting results.

80/20 Lean Cart

This isn't about being perfect - it's about progress. Easy fix: We make it a habit to fill the large part of our family's grocery cart with wholesome, nutrient-dense edibles like vegetables, fruits, low-fat dairy, lean meats, and whole grains, and reserve the small section at the top of the cart for one or two decadent treats.

If you're making a healthy choice 80% of the time, you'll win at being lean. Apply this 80/20 rule to the way you shop. That means 20% of your cart can be filled with a less healthy choice, and you'll still succeed. When you follow these principles about nutrition, which we're sharing from our personal experience and research, and you start to see and feel healthy differences in your body, you'll have the confidence to trust these strategies are true. You'll have learned how, and you will live to be lean.

Here's a healthy grocery checklist for you to follow:

HEALTHY FOODS   SHOPPING LIST

Fruits	Canned Foods	Frozen Foods	✓ Sesame Oil
✓ Apples	✓ Low Sodium Options	✓ Blueberries	✓ Walnut Oil
✓ Bananas	✓ Low Sodium Soup	✓ Carrots	
✓ Berries	✓ Marinara Sauce	✓ Chicken	**Beverages**
✓ Grapefruit	✓ Pineapple	✓ Corn	✓ 100% Fruit Juice
✓ Nectarines	✓ Pinto Beans	✓ Fish	✓ Herb Tea
✓ Oranges	✓ White Beans	✓ Fruit	✓ Sparkling Water
✓ Peaches	✓ Black Beans	✓ Green Beans	✓ Tomato Juice
✓ Pears	✓ Salmon	✓ Juice Bars	
	✓ Tuna	✓ Mixed Fruit	**Miscellaneous**
Grains	✓ Tomatoes	✓ Peas	✓ Tofu
✓ Oatmeal		✓ Vegetables	✓ Almonds
✓ Whole Grain Bread	**Dairy**	✓ Veggie Burgers	✓ Walnuts
✓ Whole Grain Cereal	✓ Butter		✓ Flax Seeds
✓ Whole Grain Pasta	✓ Cheddar Cheese	**Condiments**	✓ Mixed Nuts
	✓ Colby Cheese	✓ Honey	✓ Pecans
Meats	✓ Egg or Egg	✓ No Sugar Added	✓ Pumpkin Seeds
✓ Chicken	Substitute	Jam/Jelly	✓ Brown Rice
✓ Fish	✓ Low Fat Cottage	✓ Ketchup	✓ Garlic
✓ Lean beef	Cheese	✓ Low Fat Mayonnaise	✓ Herbs & Spices
✓ Pork Chops	✓ Low Fat Cream	✓ Low Sodium Soy	(instead of salt)
✓ Shell Fish	Cheese	Sauce	✓ Low Sodium &
✓ Steak	✓ Low Fat Milk	✓ Low-Fat Salad	Low Fat Crackers
✓ Turkey	✓ Low Fat Sour Cream	Dressing	
	✓ Mozzarella Cheese	✓ Mustard	
	✓ Low Fat Yogurt	✓ Olive Oil	
		✓ Salsa	

PROTEIN

An old dog CAN learn new tricks, if the "old dog" is willing. Most of us do not get enough or the right types of protein. Studies are now pointing to have people over the age of 55 eat more protein.

Next to water, protein is the most plentiful substance in the body. The most common conception of protein is meat. Beef, pork, poultry, cheese and eggs are good sources of protein. But, plant food such as nuts, beans, lentils and other legumes are also good sources.

Getting enough protein could be challenging - think about boomers who are either cooking for one or two people and tend to make quick, inexpensive meals such as pasta, cereal, grilled cheese, soups, frozen dinners or, even worse, skip meals and snack on empty calories like crackers and pretzels.

The bottom line is protein accounts for 20% of our body weight and helps to keep our hormones, enzymes, immune system, and very important cellular structures in balance, along with building muscle mass while improving bone density. Basically, we can't survive without proper levels of protein.

How much protein should I get daily? The recommended amount is 40 to 70 grams a day depending on your gender, age, health, and activity level. We've simplified this for you in the chart below.

The chart formula is based on the Recommended Dietary Allowance (RDA), which shows you that the minimum amount you need to be healthy is 0.8 grams per kilogram (0.36 grams per pound) of body weight per day. If you're an extremely active person you would need 1.8 grams per kilogram of body weight per day.

Whatever your goals, you need a combination of strength training, cardio exercise and a healthy diet that includes carbs and proteins.

APPROXIMATE PROTEIN INTAKE PER DAY CONSIDERING ACTIVITY LEVEL.

BODY WEIGHT LBS	LOW TO MODERATE EXERCISE	MODERATE MIXED EXERCISE	INTENSE ENDURANCE EXERCISE	INTENSE RESISTANCE EXERCISE	EXTREME INTENSE EXERCISE
88-132 (40-60 kg)	32g – 48g	40g – 60g	52g – 78g	68g – 102g	>88g–132g
133-176 (61-80 kg)	48g – 64g	60g – 80g	78g – 104g	102g – 136g	>132g–176g
177-220 (81-100 kg)	64g – 80g	80g – 100g	104g – 130g	136g – 170g	>176g–220g

Protein Chart Based on your Weight

Are there any signs that I'll recognize if I'm not getting enough protein?

Low Pro. You'll know it if you're too low with your protein intake:

- Low energy levels and fatigue

- Trouble building muscle mass

- Muscle, bone and joint pain

- Poor concentration and trouble learning

- Moodiness and mood swings

- Digestive issues/constipation

- Compromised immune system

- Heart health issues like high blood pressure and high cholesterol

- Blood sugar changes that can lead to diabetes

- A sluggish metabolism

- Trouble losing weight

- Brittle hair and nails; premature wrinkling of the skin

Your own needs might be different, of course, but to help you plan your protein, here's a quick list of protein-rich foods you can reach for:

ANIMAL SOURCES		
Food (serving)	Cal	Pro (g)
Skinless chicken *(3 ounces)*	141	28
Steak *(3 oz.)*	158	26
Roasted turkey *(3 oz.)*	135	25
Lamb *(3 oz.)*	172	23
Pork *(3 oz.)*	122	22
Salmon *(3 oz.)*	155	22
Tuna *(3 oz.)*	99	22
Shrimp *(3 oz.)*	101	20
Lobster *(3 oz.)*	76	16
Scallops *(3 oz.)*	75	14
EGG & DAIRY		
Food (serving)	Cal	Pro (g)
Greek yogurt *(6 oz.)*	100	18
Cottage cheese, 1% fat *(4 oz.)*	81	14
Regular yogurt, nonfat *(1 cup)*	100	11
Skim milk *(1 cup)*	86	8
Mozzarella *(1 oz.)*	72	7

PLANT SOURCES

Food (serving)	Cal	Pro (g)
Pinto beans *(½ cup)*	197	11
Lentils *(½ cup)*	101	9
Black beans *(½ cup)*	114	8
Chickpeas *(½ cup)*	134	7
Black eyed peas *(½ cup)*	100	7
Quinoa *(½ cup)*	111	4
Green peas *(½ cup)*	59	4

NUTS & SEEDS

Food (serving)	Cal	Pro (g)
Peanuts *(1 oz.)*	166	7
Peanut butter *(1 oz.)*	188	7
Almonds *(1 oz.)*	163	6
Flax seeds *(1 oz.)*	140	6
Chia seeds *(1 oz.)*	138	5

It's simple physics. At age 45, we start to lose 1% of our muscle mass each year. Adequate levels of protein help to maintain muscle mass and stamina so we can continue to feel and look younger, and have more energy.

SUGAR

As you know, sugar is damaging to your metabolism, your waistline, and your overall health. Many processed foods have added sugar. Sugar contributes to chronic inflammation, which plays a negative role in almost every function of your body.

The average American consumes 22 teaspoons of added sugar daily, which equates to almost 350 calories. Removing these added hollow calories can make a huge difference in your health, especially when it comes to losing stubborn belly fat.

One study found that eating 100 grams of sugar (the amount in two 16-ounce bottles of soda) reduced white blood cells' ability to fight bacteria by up to 50%. But while it's common knowledge that there are no actual health benefits to eating sugar, its addictive qualities make it hard to give up.

You'll be amazed how many added teaspoons of sugar are found in common foods. Brace yourself- there's lots of sneaky empty calories!

Food	Serving Size
Beverages	
Cranberry Juice Cocktail	1 cup
Lemonade	1 cup
Soda Pop	12 ounce can
Sports Drink	20 ounce bottle
Sweet Tea	1 cup
Breakfast Foods	
Breakfast Toaster Pastry	**1 pastry**
Cereal Fruit Bar	1 bar
Chocolate Puffed Cereal	1 cup
Coffee Cake	4 oz. piece
Frosted Shredded Wheat Cereal	1 cup
Glazed Doughnut	1 doughnut
Instant Sweetened Oatmeal	1 packet
Desserts	
Angel Food Cake	4 oz. piece
Brownie, No Icing	1 oz. piece
Chocolate Cake, Iced	4 oz. piece
Chocolate Chip Cookie	1 cookie
Cupcake, Iced	4 oz. piece
Gingersnaps	1 cookie
Vanilla Pudding	½ cup
Candies	
Chocolate Candy Bar	1 bar
Condiments and Sauces	
BBQ Sauce	2 tablespoons
Jam and Jelly	1 tablespoon
Ketchup	2 tablespoons
Pasta or Spaghetti Sauce	½ cup
Salad Dressing	2 tablespoons
Other Foods	
Bread, Whole Grain	1 slice
Peanut Butter	2 tablespoons
Tomato Soup	1 cup
Vanilla Yogurt	8 ounces

Added SugarTeaspoons	Added SugarGrams
7 ½ tsp	30 g
7 tsp	28 g
10 tsp	40 g
8 ½ tsp	34 g
5 ½ tsp	22 g
4 - 4 ½ tsp	**16 – 18 g**
2 ½ - 3 tsp	10 - 12 g
3 ½ tsp	14 g
5 tsp	20 g
3 tsp	12 g
4 tsp	16 g
3 tsp	12 g
7 tsp	28 g
4 tsp	16 g
10 tsp	40 g
2 tsp	8 g
6 tsp	24 g
3 tsp	12 g
5 tsp	20 g
4 ½ tsp	18 g
3 tsp	12 g
2 ½ - 3 tsp	10 – 12 g
2 tsp	8 g
2-3 tsp	8-12 g
½ - 1 tsp	2-4 g
1 tsp	4 g
¾ tsp	3 g
3 tsp	12 g
3 tsp	12 g

We also try to avoid artificial sweeteners in the ingredient list, which is in the same category as sugar.

Steer clear of the unpronounceable! Whole foods are typically easy to recognize and pronounce. Read labels! Chemicals, dyes, and preservatives tend to have long names that are hard to pronounce and often unrecognizable. It's best to steer clear of them.

Carbs. Carbs, or carbohydrates, have often been associated with weight gain. And too many people try to avoid them. We don't believe in eliminating any food group. In fact, carbs are essential for you to have energy and if want to maintain a healthy eating plan. There are two sets of carbs, healthy and 'not so' healthy.

HEALTHY "WHOLE-UNREFINED" CARBS

- Vegetables: all of them. It's best to eat a variety of vegetables every day.

- Whole fruits: apples, bananas, strawberries, etc.

- Legumes: lentils, kidney beans, peas, etc.

- Nuts: almonds, walnuts, hazelnuts, macadamia nuts, peanuts, etc.

- Seeds: chia seeds, pumpkin seeds.

- Whole grains: choose grains that are truly whole, as in pure oats, quinoa, brown rice, etc.

- Potatoes, sweet potatoes, etc.

NOT SO HEALTHY "REFINED" CARBS

- Sugary drinks: cola drinks, Vitamin water, etc. Sugary drinks are some of the unhealthiest things you can put into your body.

- Fruit juices: unfortunately, fruit juices may have similar metabolic effects as sugar-sweetened beverages.

- White bread: these are refined carbohydrates that are low in essential nutrients and bad for metabolic health. This applies to most commercially available breads.

- Pastries, cookies and cakes: these tend to be quite high in sugar and refined wheat.

- Ice cream: most types of ice cream are high in sugar, although there are exceptions.

- Candies and chocolates: If you're going to eat chocolate, choose quality dark chocolate.

- French fries and potato chips: Whole potatoes are healthy, but French fries and potato chips are not.

" The food you eat can either clean you out or plug you up."

Elaine LaLanne

Chapter 9: BOOMERS. Dining Out

J ack and Elaine ate a good number of meals outside their home and never suffered setbacks because of it. Maybe you enjoy eating out more than you used to. So, let's take a look at ways that we can incorporate eating out, while maintaining a healthy lifestyle.

The average person eats outside their home around six meals per week, which adds up to around 290 times per year and we, as consumers, want a bang for our buck. But, if we're watching our waistlines, it gets a little difficult when restaurants present our food on platters instead of dinner plates. Or, when they bring out a basketful of chips, or an assortment of bread and rolls.

Restaurants want to please us, but often our diets are demolished with their high-calorie, high-fat, and sodium-laden meals. However, we want to show you how you can navigate through any restaurant. The key is planning what to order in advance and stick to it! Decide on your priorities before going to the restaurant and avoid looking at the entire menu.

Use these tried and true suggestions the next time you step out for a meal:

Arriving

- Never go the restaurant hungry—you'll find yourself nibbling on everything that comes your way.

- Avoid "all you can eat" and buffet-style restaurants.

- "Not as healthy" preparation words: any food described as buttery, breaded, buttered, fried, pan-fried, creamed, scalloped, au gratin, a la mode.

- Avoid sauces made with milk, cheese, oil or mayonnaise. Marinara and tomato-based sauces are usually more flavorful and healthier than creamy sauces and gravies. As a rule of thumb, red is usually better than white or yellow. Get all sauces, gravies and creams on the side so you can add to taste.

- Select a meal for its protein. Aim for 15-30 grams of clean protein.

- Eat slowly! Put your fork down between bites. It takes the stomach about 20 minutes to realize that it's full.

- Watch the alcohol—it's loaded with calories, and can lower your defenses against food, causing you to eat more.

- For pasta selections, choose a marinara sauce instead of a white or red cream sauce.

- Healthy preparation words: any food described as grilled, baked, steamed, broiled, poached, stir-fried, roasted or blackened.

Appetizers

- Order a healthy appetizer, salad, or small-sized entrée as your meal.

- Replace butter or salad dressing with olive oil - that's another huge calorie savings, and brings an immense difference in terms of health benefits.

- Beware of the breadbasket. It comes early and can be refilled several times. Ask that it be brought only with the meal and limit yourself to one serving.

- If you're going to have a piece of bread before the meal, then we would advise not to order something that is "bready" like a sandwich or pizza.

- Instead of having a main meal, it's OK to order 2 healthy appetizers in one sitting. This can provide a healthy advantage as the portions are smaller and you have a variety of nutritious choices.

- Select white chicken or turkey meat rather than dark meat, and have the skin removed.

- Gain an edge on hunger by starting with a broth-based soup, raw vegetables, or a light seafood appetizer.

Meal

- Split the entrée in half and ask for a side salad. If alone, ask for the entrée to be divided in half and packaged in a carryout before it comes to the table.

- Avoid foods that have been prepared in heavy cream.

- Foods that are grilled, baked, steamed, or broiled, provide healthy, flavorful alternatives. Ask how an entrée is prepared to ensure that your selection is not drenched in butter or other fattening sauce.

- Trim all visible fat from your red meat.

- Order imaginative whole-grain side dishes like bulgur or kasha instead of white rice or pasta.

- Choose whole-grain versions of pasta and bread; substitute whole-wheat flour for bleached white flour when you bake.

- Have a meal that comes with condiments on the side, not already dressed. This alone can save you 200-plus calories.

- Order a meal that has grains like quinoa or brown rice instead of potatoes, but order potatoes instead of breads and pastas.

- Decrease the meat and increase the vegetables called for in stews and casseroles.

Desserts

- Eat your dessert—but make it a treat, not a ritual. Use a 3-bite rule for desserts: Notice we didn't say don't have a dessert. You can take three bites of the most decadent dessert and still control calories. You'll find that those 3 bites are really the most satisfying, and afterwards, you're not even tasting the dessert anymore.

Dining In:

- Cook with less fat by using non-stick skillets.

- Blot all fried meats on paper towels. Or better yet, try baking or broiling instead of frying.

- Avoid cooking with Soy or Worcestershire sauce and products that contain monosodium glutamate (MSG).

- Use garlic or onion powder instead of garlic or onion salt, and use unsalted or low-salt vegetable broths and products.

- Buy reduced-fat cheese or use mozzarella, which is naturally lower in fat.

- In recipes calling for milk or cream, substitute reduced fat versions or try using other "milks" such as rice milk, nut milk, or soy milk. Also use low-fat cream cheese, yogurt, and mayo.

- Unhealthy fats like certain oils, butter, or margarines can usually be cut by 1/3 to 1/2 in recipes. At first, try a small reduction and then use less and less over time; you'll hardly notice the difference.

- You can also use fat substitutes like prune purees and applesauce in baked goods.

- Use fresh-frozen fruit without added sugar if fresh is unavailable.

- Cut the sugar called for in most recipes by 1/3 to 1/2.

- Sweeten waffles and quick breads with cinnamon, cardamom, vanilla or almond extracts in order to cut the sugar content.

- Try salsa on a baked potato or salad rather than high-fat dressing or butter.

Chapter 10: BOOMERS. Recipes

I f you need some ideas for delicious healthy recipes, we've included some in this book. All the recipes have 8 ingredients or less and promote good health. These are created by nutritionist, Dani Spies, and with her permission, we offer them here for you. For more of Dani's delectable treats go to her site… www.cleananddelicious.com.

Bon Appetit!

8 Ingredients ...or Less

BREAKFAST RECIPES

HIGH PROTEIN BLUEBERRY PANCAKES

1 cup of rolled oats
6 egg whites (3/4 cup)
1 cup of low-fat cottage cheese
½ teaspoon of vanilla extract
½ teaspoon cinnamon
2 teaspoons honey
½ cup of blueberries

DIRECTIONS:

Combine all of the ingredients (except for the blueberries) in a blender and blend until everything is well combined (about 30 seconds). You want to have a nice smooth "pancake batter-like" consistency.

Gently stir in the blueberries.

Pre heat a non-stick pan or griddle over a medium heat and lightly coat with cooking spray. Scoop ¼ cup of the batter on to the hot pan. Repeat, adding as many pancakes as you can without crowding the pan. Cook for about three minutes or until the edges start to bubble. Flip the pancakes and cook for another two minutes or until golden brown.

Top with maple syrup, fruit, or my personal favorite; almond butter!

Makes 2 servings.

BROCCOLI + CHEESE SCRAMBLE

1 teaspoon coconut oil
½ cup broccoli, chopped
1 egg + 1/3 cup egg whites
1 tablespoon shredded cheddar cheese
Salt and pepper to taste

DIRECTIONS:

Heat a small, non-stick sauté pan over a medium heat. Melt the coconut oil and then add in broccoli. Season with salt and pepper and cook for 3-5 minutes or until the broccoli is tender.

In the meantime, whisk the egg and egg whites together. Pour the egg mixture over the broccoli and stir frequently until the eggs are just about set.

Sprinkle cheese over the top, shut off the heat and pop on a lid for a couple of minutes or until the cheese has melted. Serve and enjoy!

Serves 1 (can easily be scaled up for more servings)

LUNCH RECIPES

TURKEY VEGGIE SAMMIE ON A PEPPER BUN

1 bell pepper
1 piece red leaf lettuce
1-2 roasted peppers (from a jar)
2 ounces organic turkey breast
1 ounce cheddar cheese, thinly sliced
5 spicy pickle slices
1/4 cup hummus

DIRECTIONS:

Slice off the cheeks from your pepper and use the two biggest halves for the bread.

On top of one pepper cheek, layer red leaf lettuce, roasted pepper, turkey, cheddar cheese, and pickles.

Spread the hummus on the remaining pepper cheek and place on top to create a sandwich.

Serve and enjoy!

Makes 1 sandwich.

QUINOA SPINACH + MANGO BOWL

2 big handfuls baby spinach, chopped
1 clove garlic, crushed
1/2 cup COOKED quinoa
1/3 cup chopped yellow pepper
1/3 cup chopped mango
Juice from 1/2 lime
salt and pepper to taste

DIRECTIONS:

Combine baby spinach, garlic, quinoa, pepper, and mango in a medium bowl. Top with lime juice, salt and pepper. Gently toss and enjoy!

DINNER RECIPES

ONE PAN ROASTED CHICKEN + VEGGIES

6 boneless, skinless chicken thighs
1 lb. baby potatoes, slice in half
2 bell peppers, cut into both size chunks
1 red or yellow onion, cut into bite size pieces
1 tablespoon olive oil
2 teaspoon smoked paprika
2 teaspoon garlic powder
1/2 teaspoon kosher salt + sprinkle of black pepper

DIRECTIONS:

Pre oven to 425 °F

Line a rimmed baking sheet with aluminum foil and lightly coat with some cooking spray.

Lay chicken out on the pan and the surround it with the potatoes, bell peppers, and onions doing your best not to have them overlap on one and other.

Drizzle the olive oil over the chicken and veggie and then season with smoked paprika, garlic powder, salt and pepper.

Pop in the oven for 30 minutes or until the veggie are tender and the chicken is cooked through. Serve and enjoy!

Makes 4 servings.

BROCCOLI + BROWN RICE QUESADILLAS

1 whole grain tortilla
1/3 cup part skim shredded cheese (any type you like)
¼ cup COOKED brown rice
¼ cup steamed broccoli (or any leftover veggie you have on hand)
¼ teaspoon garlic powder
pinch of Kosher salt

DIRECTIONS:

Heat a medium non-stick sauté pan over a medium-high heat. Add tortilla and warm up for about 15 seconds, then flip.

Layer half the cheese on half of the tortilla and top with brown rice and broccoli. Layer the remaining cheese over the rice and broccoli, then season with garlic powder and salt.

Fold the tortilla over onto itself and place a heavy pot or teapot on top for 30 seconds. Flip the tortilla and cook for another 30 seconds, or until cheese has melted and tortilla is browned and crispy.

Serve with your favorite toppings. Enjoy!

Makes 1 serving.

DESSERT RECIPES

3-INGREDIENT BANANA OATMEAL COOKIES

1.5 cups oatmeal (I used 1/2 cup rolled and 1 cup quick)
2 medium bananas
1/3 cup mini chocolate chips

DIRECTIONS:

Preheat oven to 350 degrees Fahrenheit.

Line a rimmed baking sheet with a silpat mat or coat with some cooking spray.

Using the back of a fork, mash bananas in a medium bowl until they are broken down. Add in oats and gently stir until all of the oats and bananas are mixed together and look like a thick cookie batter.

Now you're ready to add the chocolate chips! Sprinkle them into the dough and stir until they are just mixed throughout.

Scoop one heaping tablespoon of the dough into your hands and free form into a cookie*. Place on cookie sheet and continue until you have 12 cookies.

Cook for 12-15 minutes or until set through and lightly golden. Cool and enjoy!

*NOTE: these cookies will not spread in the oven so be sure to form them into a cookie before placing on baking sheet.

Makes 15 cookies.

SECRET INGREDIENT CHOCOLATE MOUSE

1 avocado, peeled and pitted
¼ cup cocoa powder
2 tablespoons maple syrup of honey
½ teaspoon vanilla extract
½ cup unsweetened vanilla almond milk

DIRECTIONS:

Place avocado into a food processor and blend until the avocado breaks down a bit.

Add cocoa powder, maple syrup and vanilla; blend again until you have a nice smooth consistency.

Add in the almond milk to thin out the mixture a bit. Blend until everything is well incorporated.

Chill in the fridge for a couple of hours. Enjoy!

Makes 4 servings.

APPETIZER RECIPES

SHORT CUT BRUSCHETTA HUMMUS

1 cup chopped tomatoes (buy the most beautiful, in season tomatoes you can find)
1-2 cloves crushed garlic
5 basil leaves, finely chopped
1 teaspoon balsamic vinegar
1 teaspoon extra virgin olive oil
Salt and pepper to taste
10 ounce container or your favorite hummus

DIRECTIONS:

In small bowl, combine tomatoes, garlic, basil, vinegar, olive oil, salt and pepper. Gently toss until well combined.

Transfer hummus into your favorite serving dish and top with tomato mixture.

Serve with fresh veggies and pita chips. Enjoy!

MAPLE WRAPPED BRUSSEL SPROUTS

10 medium to large brussels sprouts, trimmed and halved
5 pieces of nitrate free bacon
1-2 tablespoons maple syrup
black pepper

DIRECTIONS:

Pre heat oven to 425°F and line a rimmed baking sheet with parchment paper or a silpat mat.

Slice each side of bacon in half horizontally and then slice each half in half again, vertically. You will end up with 4 thin strips of bacon when done.

Brush each slice of bacon with the maple syrup. Wrap the bacon around the brussels sprouts and place on the baking sheet. Repeat until you have finished wrapping all the brussels sprouts in bacon.

Brush the tops of the bacon wrapped sprouts with some more maple syrup and season with black pepper.

Pop in the oven for thirty minutes or until the bacon has cooked and brussels sprouts are tender. Serve and enjoy!

Makes 20 brussels sprout bites.

Borrowed Wisdom: On Excuses

Please don't use time as an explanation for not getting fit. You make time for all the things you want to do – remember, that's "want power". If you really want to get in better shape, then you must use your "want power." If you want to go to the movie you make time. There is always something you can do, even if it's a little bit at a time. This is the simple choice each of us must make on a daily basis - and don't forget, only 8 minutes can change your life. More reps aren't always better. A longer interval isn't necessarily better than a short one. Be consistent and you will succeed.

~Jaime

Today is your day. This is the first day of the rest of your Life. You're going to stay consistent. You're going to keep going. You're not going to give up. And, you're never going to look back. So, keep your ARC of Life over your head:

A= Living life with a positive **Attitude**;

R= Use **Resistance** to induce muscle strength and resist the food undermining your health;

C= Be **Consistent** in your workouts and in your diet.

If you want to have more Energy... Move

If you want increased Vitality... Move

If you want optimum Performance... Move

If you want to stay Healthy, Fit, and Strong... Move

If you want to regain your Fountain of Youth... Move

If you want to bring a Smile to your face... Move

IF YOU WANT TO LIVE, MOVE!!

Jaime and his wife, Teri, working out together.

Chapter 11: BOOMERS. Habits created – lives changed!

Listen to what others are saying...

Gayle S. *67 year old* - I really want to express how much I like Jaime's videos. I've been involved in sports, majored in PE in college, broke a NCAA track record, martial arts 5-time world champion, so I've seen a lot of fitness programs etc. Jaime's videos are the most fun, motivating, easy to follow and the exercise works. The exercises are simple and effective and the sequence of these really work. I haven't found anything better.

Jim V. *58 year old* – Fifteen months ago I felt tired and weak. I was also 15 lbs. overweight. I couldn't stay consistent with any exercise or diet plan I was putting myself on, so I decided to give Jaime Brenkus a call at Lean Living. Jaime and I talked about a proper diet and he said what I needed at my age was to build lean muscle, eat properly and burn more fat. He said I had to commit to at least two workouts a week and he would hold me accountable to my diet. I agreed, and we got started. A few weeks into the program, I started to see and feel the difference. I truly felt better and did have more energy.

At 3 months I was in better shape than I had been in for 30 yrs. I was feeling great both physically and mentally, and then I had a routine checkup and 30 days later was diagnosed with Prostate Cancer. I went through radiation treatment and was given a shot that wiped out my testosterone for 9 months. I continued working out with Jaime while in treatment. There were times when I wanted to give up, but Jaime kept encouraging me and each time I worked out, I actually felt better. If I hadn't gotten that 3 month head start on my health and fitness program, I would have never done so well with the treatment.

I am now 6 months out of treatment, continuing my wellness program and feeling great! I would recommend to everyone male or female, start eating better and exercise. I started again at 57 and 15 months later I feel more energized, my clothes fit better and I am more confident. I also stopped having to take cholesterol medicine and blood pressure pills. As Jaime would say "Nothing tastes better than lean feels."

John V - Jaime Brenkus was very, very instrumental in helping me "recover" my body. I am 76 years old and have always been very athletically active. I have been rowing on an indoor Concept II machine for the last 15 years. 2 1/2 years ago I tore my hamstrings while rowing (due to not properly stretching before and after rowing). As a result, I could not row or exercise for 5 months and my muscles atrophied to the point that I could not even lift a half gallon of milk. I went to the Cleveland Clinic and was not happy with their rehab program. Finally, I consulted with Jaime and showed him a picture of when my body was really "cut". I told Jaime that was how I wanted to look again. Thanks to God and to Jaime's fantastic rehab program I am very happy to say, "My body's back".

Chuck A -Thanks to Jaime Brenkus, I have lost 29 pounds in the past 6 weeks. More importantly, my Doctor was astonished at the difference in my numbers. My cholesterol went from 246 to 172. My LDL went from 179 down to 119, my HDL went up three notches from 32 to 35. The most dramatic change was my Triglycerides --going from 193 down to 51.

Robert, Alabama - For years I said, "I would start my diet on Monday!" Well Monday never came, and I gained over 100 pounds! Starting at 367 in just 7 weeks I have lost 35 pounds with Jaime's Plan. I get to eat six (6) meals a day, I am never hungry, and I am still losing an average of 5 pounds a week. My first goal was 60 pounds, but now I have my eye on 117 pounds which will take me back to my high school years when I played football (don't tell anyone that was over 35 years ago). I know I will be healthier. My glucose has dropped over 120 points and my blood pressure is a calm 120/70! Thanks Jaime for helping me see my grandkids grow up.

Angela O. - I cannot recommend Jaime enough to anyone who has ever had a dream of what they CAN be. The encouragement and education I have received from Jaime and his staff are worth their weight in gold! With my incredible trainer Andrea, I have changed my body from being frumpy & middle-aged, to being strong & lean. Andrea doesn't look at this as just a job, she takes a personal interest in your success! I look forward to each & every workout I have and was amazed at the changes in my body at the age of 56! I've lost weight on ALL kinds of programs before, but NOTHING compares to building muscle in your body. It's actually fun to go clothes shopping now, and not a worry when you are invited to a cookout on a hot summer's day to show up in shorts. My only regret is I wish I would have done it 10 years ago! Run, don't walk to Jaime's plan if you are tired of sitting and dreaming about a fit life, and really want to live that life.

Donna R - I am, without a doubt, a major success story. I used to weigh 317 pounds. Thankfully, just when I thought I had reached the end of my rope, Jaime Brenkus came into my life. I went on his program and within the first month, I lost 20 pounds. Now, a little over a year later, I have lost an amazing 158 pounds. I have gone from a dress size 28 to 16. If I can do it, I know you can too!

Elizabeth C. - I started out about 5 months ago when the doctor told me "lose some weight, you're pre-diabetic". Since hearing those words, I have lost 26 pounds and 20 inches, and have gone from a size 18-20 to a size 10. I have been able to do this successfully by using the portion plate and workouts. I never thought I'd love to work out, but now I can't wait. Thank you, Jaime!

Pam S. - "During the past four months of working with Jaime, I lost 43 pounds and 40 inches, and went from size 16 to size 9. What an exciting accomplishment this was for me. I feel great. My clothes are all too big! This weight loss also led to reduction in my current pressure medicine. I am now discussing with the doctor the possibility of getting off the cholesterol and pressure medicine all together. Losing this weight has given me a whole new way of thinking. I no longer beat myself up about being fat! I learned portion control and how to incorporate into my daily life. I am eating much healthier now and plan to continue to eat this way for the rest of my life. The training I received with Jaime was not only physical but mental too! This training will help me for the rest of my life not just the 4 months that I was losing weight. I'm not sure how they did it, but I actually like to exercise now. Something is just not right in my day if I don't fit in a little cardio or weight training into it. The nice thing is it's not hours and hours of work each day, it is a reasonable amount of time that I can fit into my schedule. "

Maura S. - I have worked out with Jaime Brenkus as my Fitness Trainer. Being an avid runner for years, I was looking for ways to improve my program, Jaime's unique approach to fitness by combining cardio and resistance exercises, has allowed me to decrease my running time and stave off any leg injuries that may have occurred in the past. I feel so much lighter on my feet now that I've lost over 45 pounds, and a remarkable 46 inches, while dropping down 4 pant sizes. He has taught me how to properly fuel my body for my weekly runs, and my marathon races. With 45 pounds lost and my muscles stronger, I have become so much faster and more efficient in my running. Thank you, Jaime.

Dr. Michael S. Tampa, FL - Following Jaime's program, I lost 40 pounds. It's the only approach that gave me long term results.

Barbara M. - I've been 49 for a few years now. As a wife, businessperson, someone involved in charitable causes, and now the mom of a 7-year old with special needs, my physical wellbeing had taken a back seat. I had a plethora

155

of excuses from too much work, too tired, too this, too that! I tried multiple diets that lasted for less than 24 hours and spurts of manic exercise routines that last about as long as the diet. I didn't eat breakfast, barely ate lunch and ate the wrong things at night. It wasn't until I committed myself to Jaime's Program did I start to get results with common sense initiatives. Eating breakfast, watching portions and exercise. But it was the commitment to my appointments with Jaime that made it happen. Being accountable to Jaime makes you want to do the right thing – eat right and think lean. I don't always succeed in the eating department all the time, but I'm encouraged not to feel guilty about those slips and I have seen incredible results – including my cholesterol dropping 101 points in 3 months. I will never be like I was in my 20's, but I feel healthy, energized, less stressed and happy about my improved appearance.

Sharnette R. - Seeing is believing! In just over 3 months, I have lost 24 lbs. and approximately 20 overall inches. Words cannot express the feeling of stepping out of those size 14 jeans and easing into those 9/10's that had been sitting on the shelf collecting dust. And I did this without some crazy diet or starving myself. At 47 years old, I can honestly say I'm in the best shape of my life and look forward to living a strong and healthy future. I look in the mirror and I love this woman who is looking back at me!!! With the support, encouragement and awesome workouts from Jaime, and Andrea, I changed my lifestyle with proper nutrition and portion control, positive thinking, moving forward and NEVER giving up. I wouldn't trade this for anything and I will always be grateful for making that initial phone call to Jaime that changed my life.

Ginny M. - I was diagnosed with pre-diabetes, placed on medications and was instructed on how to check my glucose. My physician encouraged me to lose weight and exercise as a means of controlling my glucoses. Since I was struggling to lose weight and exercise independently, I started on a journey, by signing on with Jaime's program, and having a personal trainer; Andrea… she is a "gem." She knows when to push and when to back off, and is always encouraging. It has been nine months now, and I am down 43 pounds, and 31 inches including 9 inches from my waist. My overall health has improved… I can walk up a flight of stairs without getting short of breath, my energy level has increased dramatically and to top it all off, my glucose levels are running at the lower end of normal! Just this week, Andrea had me jogging on the treadmill at 4.7 mph…now that was for only a minute and a half, but I never thought I would be able to do it.

William S. M., M.D. Obesity in America has reached epidemic proportions, afflicting one third of adults and one fourth of children. In addition to the obvious emotional and psychological trauma it inflicts, obesity can lead to a myriad of life-threatening conditions, including diabetes, high blood pressure, heart disease, sleep disorders, osteoarthritis, and certain types of cancer. However, the good news is that obesity is preventable in 99+ % of people. The Slim & Fit weight loss system and Jaime's trademarked Fusion workout offers my patients the most advanced personal weight loss system in America. Based on proven food science and simple body physics, Slim & Fit works every time."

Matt H. St. Paul Minn. -Dear Jack, I want to thank you for not only greatly helping me in my health and fitness but for saving my life. After reading your book my wife realized I was almost like your father had been. I am 50 years old, a father of 12 children, and grandfather of four.

Six months ago, I was obese, sickly, always tired and could not even walk up the stairs to my living room without resting. I would even fall asleep at my desk job and sometimes would even have to pull over driving during the day. I had no strength left after work to do anything with my wife or children. My wife strongly encouraged me to see a doctor because I was always thirsty. Off course I had type two diabetes. Looking back, I probably wouldn't have lived to e 60. The doctor put me on diabetes medications and blood pressure pills. I was finally scared enough to do something drastic in my life. I started slowly with exercise (walking) and went on a low carb diabetic diet, but I knew I needed a permanent change if I wanted to see if my children grow up. I remembered your diet/exercise advice and knew of your great health, strength and longevity. I began to incorporate your plans with my diet and exercise. It was tough at first to get rid of the old cravings, I can't believe I lived like that. But slowly my tastes and desire changed and at first, I made changes in stages, as I gave up what was bad for me and started eating what was right. Over the past six month I have become a new man. I have lost nearly 70 pounds and 10 inches off my waist I never go hungry, I eat food the way God made it, 'If man made it don't eat it'. Instead of resting half way up the stairs I run up. I can play with my kids again. I work out at a health club 5 to 6 days a week, and I can exercise like I was 25 years younger.

I must admit that I didn't expect the results to be this amazing and I have gone off the medications and I am discussing with my doctor the possibility of reducing or eliminating the blood pressure medications. I no long miss or want the garbage I use d to eat. One of my daughters told me she wants to go your life style plan completely. I want you to know you were a messenger from God and made the biggest difference in my life by teaching and openly living what really works. Thanks so much for your help.

Frank A. -Dear Elaine and Jack, Thanks for all your inspiration in helping America stay fit and healthy. I hope we can slow the progression of obesity and lack of fitness that still plagues our society.

Sandy E.-Dear Elaine and Jack, I'm so happy to have the CDs of your shows. I like the way you say beginner stop. It's great to have you Elaine and your dog Happy in my living room. The one I have now is Forever Young (to be that would something) I like the way you motivate us.

Shirley G. -Dear Jack and Elaine, If you ever need a testimonial I'm it. I'm 75 years old and a truly proven example of you exercise and diet programs. At 60 I started a modeling career and in demand for fashion and runway modeling in Florida. I am now embarking on a career of motivational speaking. I believe what you always say. "Anything is life is possible if you make it happen".

Gus O Commander USN, Retired-Dear Jack! I was at my spinning class this morning and my mind wandered into the reason why I am thankful as we approach Thanksgiving. One thing that I am thankful for is my health and a major influence in maintaining a healthy life style is you..I remember as a kid growing up seeing you on TV with your German

Sheppard and you would always pop up in the news when you would set a record while swimming the Golden Gate or from Alcatraz. You were always gracious and good natured and an inspiration. So this Thanksgiving I am thankful for many things, one of them is for You.

David, Navy CDR, Retired - Dear Jack and Elaine LaLanne, My name is David. I'm a recently retired Navy CDR. I'm not anyone of any special notoriety, and I don't have any hidden agenda. I'm sure you get countless letters like this, but I just wanted to add my two cents in, to let you know how much I, and many others like myself, appreciate the wonderful example you two have been to the citizens of our country for so many years. We have all benefitted from your physical, patriotic and spiritual examples. I know that you have been purposeful in setting these examples, and then you have actually followed through and lived them. That is unusual, remarkable and worthy of, at very least, our appreciation. So, thank you both very much. I don't know your particular religious beliefs, but I am sure the Lord is also proud of your diligent service.

General Foods -Elaine is an enthusiastic motivator. She does her utmost to make it happen

Agency for Post Natural Bran Flakes- People flock to her! Elaine even gets the most jaded people up and moving.

Point of purchase Advertising Institute-Your enthusiasm and energy were catching, we heard nothing but rave reviews on the women's program.

Dept. of Public Health, City& County of San Francisco-Your presence sparked a lot of enthusiasm for the 2000 walkers who attended the event, you were the highlight.

Kellie Kaseburg, Senior Director of Events, IDEA Health and Fitness Association- Dear Elaine, Thank you SO MUCH for everything you did to make IDEA World so special this year!! You are the most amazing person ever – so inspiring and full of life! Thank you for helping us to carry out our mission to Inspire the World to Fitness! I can't wait to see you next year at the IDEA Convention in San Diego!

Thanks again and take care!

Borrowed Wisdom: On Doubt

"I can't do this. I can't stick with that, there's no way I can live like this the rest of my life." These words can tear us apart. Is it your desire to hold up your progression towards a healthy lifestyle? The best saboteur of your goals is to have doubt. Yet doubt is nothing but a thought and has no power other than the power you give to it. You have the authority and control to let go of this albatross. Any doubt, with a little mental effort, can be vanished the very second you want it to.

It's your choice! When you let doubt go, it falls away from you and rapidly dribbles into nothing. There's not one single doubt that is permanently affixed to you. Fill your mental computer chip with positive, empowering confidence that you can and will make the necessary changes for life lasting health. There's a solution for everything, if you want one! Let it go, it's gone!

~Jaime

Chapter 12: Jack and Elaine's Journey

Y ou can't be married to Jack and not learn from him. He was an expert in human anatomy and physiology. He opened the very first modern health club called Jack LaLanne's Physical Culture Studio in 1936. He invented the leg extension machine, the first weight selector, the squat machine, later the Smith machine, redesigned by his good friend Rudy Smith. The wrist roll and the calf machine were also his designs. You will see these concepts in most of the equipment today.

Jack doing squats on the machine he invented

Many will remember his five day a week Jack LaLanne exercise show on national television which lasted for 34 years.

Jack getting the crew in shape on the set of his TV show

Many will remember too (because Jack wanted to show the world that you don't have to be 'over the hill' if you are 40, 50, 60, or even 70 or 80), how he would perform a feat to show that - if you are in shape - "anything in life is possible and you can make it happen."

In his 40s, he swam from Alcatraz Island in San Francisco to Fisherman's Wharf handcuffed. In his 60s he swam handcuffed and ankles shackled towing a 1,000 pound boat, from Alcatraz to San Francisco. When he was 70 years old, he towed 70 people in 70 boats, wrist and ankles cuffed, a mile and half in Long Beach harbor along the Queen Mary mile ending up at the ship, The Queen Mary.

See more about Jack LaLanne's life: www.jacklalanne.com

Jack pulling 70 boats in San Francisco at 70 years old

As mentioned, I was a professed junk food junkie. I knew nothing about nutrition or working out. I was born in 1926 and raised during the depression and WWII years in Minneapolis, Minnesota. The bread, butter, cream, sugar and salt always had to be on the table. I was in pretty good shape in the 1940s having been a ballet swimmer. However, I had moved to California in 1946 and until 1951, I did no exercise and my nutrition habits were the pits.

Television was in its early stages. My career in TV began in 1948 when television was in its infancy and the first broadcast was at 6 p.m. in the evening where I did a bread commercial. When television eventually came on at 4:30 in the afternoon

I landed a job as a Girl Friday (co-host today) with a local radio personality, Les Malloy. The show was on from 4:30 to 6 pm. We had a 12-piece orchestra from the radio days. I appeared and booked all the guests on the 90-minute show.

Elaine working on the Les Malloy show in 1948

I remember receiving a phone call one afternoon, "We've got this guy who can do pushups through your hour and a half show." Wow! That sounded great. It was Jack LaLanne! A couple of weeks later he appeared on the nationwide Art Baker "You Asked for It" TV show where he did 1,033 push-ups in 23 minutes. The next thing I know, Jack was on the air with an exercise show in 1951.

I was smoking, eating poorly (candy bars for lunch) with no exercise. Jack began an exercise class at noon. He was so dynamic and convincing that I quit smoking, changed my eating habits, began to exercise every day and within weeks I felt better, had more energy and the exercise was firming up my flab. I changed a few bad habits for good ones and you can, too. From that point, I was hooked on a new way of life.

We went on to develop the first "Instant Breakfast" protein drink and nutrition bar, the first resistance stretchers called the Glamour Stretcher and Easy Way for men. See Jack's website for his videos and for more firsts: www.jacklalanne.com.

Jack and Elaine motivating viewers all over the country

Through the years Jack and I toured the country, lecturing and motivating people to get off their seat and on to the feet!

Jack giving a lecture holding 3 pounds of fat

Jack speaking at one of his lectures to a full house

Jack teaching kids to get fit...starting them young !

I've written five books; Dynastride, Eating Right for a New You, Fitness After 50, Fitness After 50 Workout and Total Juicing. I toured the country for General Foods Post Natural Bran Flakes and also toured the country promoting my books. I've not only appeared on all the Jack LaLanne shows, but also on the Power and Fusion Juicer infomercials, and have made appearances on countless television programs such as The Today Show, The Early Show, Good Morning America, Fox and Friends, Tony Danza, Howard Stern and many, many more.

The Dynamic duo, Jack and Elaine, photos taken 30 years apart

Today in my nineties I haven't slowed down and can still do full body pushups. Traveling and meeting thousands of people from all over, I've heard so many stories of how people have turned their lives around by wanting to, believing they can, and following through with their goals and I know you can do it too!

Elaine LaLanne
(Now you know all about me)

Elaine doing pushups in her 90's.

We hope that you will enjoy your journey into a new you!

-Jaime and Elaine

Printed in Great Britain
by Amazon

31258618R00106